THE COMPLETE BOOK OF
NORTH AMERICAN
BUTTERFLIES

THE COMPLETE BOOK OF
NORTH AMERICAN
BUTTERFLIES

EDITED BY PAUL A. OPLER

THUNDER BAY
P · R · E · S · S

San Diego, California

Thunder Bay Press
An imprint of the Baker & Taylor Publishing Group
10350 Barnes Canyon Road, San Diego, CA 92121
www.thunderbaybooks.com

Produced by Salamander Books,
an imprint of Anova Books Company Ltd.,
10 Southcombe Street, London W14 0RA, U.K.

All notations of errors or omissions should be addressed to Thunder Bay Press,
Editorial Department, at the above address. All other correspondence (author
inquiries, permissions) concerning the content of this book should be addressed
to Salamander Books, 10 Southcombe Street, London W14 0RA, U.K.

Library of Congress Cataloging-in-Publication Data available upon request.

Printed in China.

1 2 3 4 5 15 14 13 12 11

Endpapers: Old World swallowtail (*Papilio machaon*). Photo: Darrell Gulin/Corbis.
Page 2: Long-tailed skipper (*Urbanus proteus*). Photo: Richard Skoonberg.

Contents

Introduction

Opposite: The Arcas Cattleheart (*Parides arcas mylotes*) is very similar to the ruby-spotted swallowtail, a visitor to southern Texas.
Below: The Marcella daggerwing (*Marpesia marcella*) with its distinctive tails. The most common daggerwing seen in the United States is the ruddy daggerwing.

Butterflies are among the most easily recognizable of all animals. Their wings, unlike those of most other insects, are colorful, predominantly opaque, and have a characteristic shape. Butterflies are instantly familiar and also universally popular. They seem to escape the general revulsion reserved for most other insects, perhaps because they do not bite, sting, carry disease, or (in the adult form) do any serious damage.

Certainly their popularity is due largely to their appearance. Many butterflies are among the most gorgeous creatures, noted for their glorious colors. It is worth remembering that while we take color for granted, in the animal kingdom it is the exception and not the rule. The

Above: A vivid trio of great spangled fritillaries (*Speyeria cybele*), feeding on the nectar of milkweed flowers.

Opposite: The distinctive colors of the ruddy daggerwing (*Marpesia petreus*). This butterfly is active year-round in southern Florida and lays its eggs on the leaves of fig trees.

development of color, its range, diversity, brilliance, and the kaleidoscope of patterns exhibited by butterflies is unrivaled anywhere in the animal world, except possibly by birds. Color is not just a form of eye-catching advertisement, but may also be used for camouflage and defense.

Butterflies are typically active during the day. This is another important factor drawing them to our attention because it not only ensures that their colors will be fully appreciated, but this activity contrasts sharply with the behavior of a great majority of animals that are nocturnal. It is therefore hardly surprising that butterflies have been so popular among collectors, observers, and photographers.

However, to see butterflies merely as pretty objects is to miss half the story, for they are of exceptional interest in many other ways. The wings of these insects are emblazoned with the evidence of their ancestry, like the quarterings on the shields of ancient nobles. This feature makes them

fine subjects for an investigation of the ways in which all living things evolve. Moreover, the selective breeding of races and forms has revealed some of the complexities involved in the mechanism of evolution. The results of these studies may in some cases be of direct benefit to ourselves.

Perhaps the most dramatic example of such a benefit is the advance made in combating rhesus disease, one of the major causes of infant mortality. The way in which this disease is transmitted to the unborn child was initially suggested by unrelated research into the genetics of the African swallowtail (*Papilio dardanus*). Other butterflies, or their early stages, are used in the study of cancers, anemia, and viral infections.

Because butterflies are so skilled in flight, they have achieved an almost worldwide distribution, though as with most animal groups (particularly cold-blooded ones), there is a greater diversity to be found in the tropics. However, a butterfly can fly only so far, and there is a very clear separation between the butterflies that live in widely separated continental landmasses. In North America, the Rocky Mountains provide both a barrier to east–west movement and a unique habitat. Alpine meadows—flat grassland above 6,500 feet—are

Right: The painterly qualities of the Rocky Mountain Parnassian (*Parnassius smintheus*), photographed in June near the Cascade–Siskiyou National Monument in Oregon.

uncommon in the Rockies, but many have rare butterfly populations. Long-term research in the Alberta Rockies indicates that trees present a significant barrier to butterfly movement, and that Rocky Mountain Parnassians will actively avoid flying into forested areas. Thus, if the area surrounding their alpine meadow is forested, once their habitat begins to shrink, they do not have the ability to move out and find new meadows beyond.

The butterfly life cycle is no less remarkable than the beauty of the adult. The transformation of the sometimes ugly and often bizarre caterpillar into an elegant butterfly is one of the regularly performed

Above: Mitchell's satyr (*Neonympha mitchellii*) is now confined to isolated areas in Michigan, Alabama, and North Carolina. There were populations in Ohio and New Jersey, but development of its habitats extinguished any trace of this rare satyr.

miracles of nature. This natural conjuring trick of turning beast into beauty also includes an ecological subtlety: the larva and the adult are able to lead totally different lifestyles, thus enabling these two stages of the life cycle to avoid competing with each other for the same food.

Sadly, butterflies are threatened by habitat destruction almost everywhere. Some of the richest areas for wildlife are being cleared and planted with agricultural crops. In others, the traditional methods of grazing and land management have changed, reducing the diversity of plant species. Even if butterflies could survive in the new habitat, their larvae probably would not, because of the loss of their specific food

Above: A tropical jewel, the malachite (*Siproeta stelenes*) is only resident in southern Texas and southern Florida, occasionally straying north. From a butterfly watcher's perspective, Arizona, Texas, and Florida offer the greatest range of spectacular butterflies in the United States.

plants. If they took to feeding on the crops instead, they would then be deliberately destroyed as pests. It is no use protecting butterflies because they are attractive unless we take even greater care to conserve their larvae and the places where they live.

The first part of this book attempts to show not only what the butterfly is, but also how it comes to be that way and what it does. The second part aims to illustrate the traditionally recognized family groups of butterflies in North America, showing similarity and diversity within the family and also how each differs from the next.

The arrangement of these families, and indeed their basic validity as natural groups, has been questioned, and perhaps here again butterflies deserve to be singled out. In no other group of animals has the scientific nomenclature been so thoroughly bedeviled by a profusion of names, revisions, and repeated attempts to sort out the confusion.

Below: The bulky abdomen of a mangrove skipper (*Phocides pigmalion*) helps demonstrate the huge variation in shapes of butterflies. Mangrove skippers feed on red mangrove plants and are limited to the coastal margins of Florida.

Lepidoptera

About three-quarters of all described animal species are insects. Their present-day abundance and diversity of form suggest a long and complex evolutionary history. In some orders of insects, at least part of this history may be traced by the study of fossils, but butterflies are delicate creatures whose bodies are likely to disintegrate immediately after death and be lost rather than preserved as fossils. Consequently, our knowledge of the history of butterflies is sketchy, and details of their ancestry remain conjectural.

Butterfly and moth fossils that show details of wing venation are usually in the form of impressions in shale deposits. These were laid down about 30 million years ago during the Oligocene epoch. In evolutionary terms this is comparatively recent, and it is thus hardly

Below: A rare survivor of the Cretaceous period (100–146 million years ago), this moth fossil is from Liaoning Province in China.

surprising that these fossil butterflies are quite similar to those alive today. We are left to guess about the more primitive forms that must have lived earlier, since these insects as a whole have existed for at least 400 million years.

The great "boom" in insect evolution seems to have occurred in the lush, gloomy fern forests of the Carboniferous period (perhaps 300 million years ago), whose curious vegetation later formed our coal deposits. One of the more spectacular Carboniferous insects was the giant dragonfly *Meganeura monyi*, with a wingspan of over 25 inches. While early butterflies were not contemporary with *Meganeura monyi*, today, large dragonflies hunt butterflies among other insects.

The characteristic association of many lepidoptera with flowering plants might suggest that the two evolved alongside each other over a similar period of time. The earliest flowering plants are known from Upper Cretaceous fossils (about 90 million years old), but the wide range of families and genera already present by then strongly suggests that their origins were much earlier.

Animals are classified into groups called phyla. Each individual phylum contains creatures that are broadly similar and possess certain features in common. For example, the phylum Arthropoda includes all those animals that have jointed limbs and a hard exoskeleton. A phylum is further subdivided into classes: in this case Crustacea (crabs, lobsters, etc.) and Arachnida (spiders, scorpions, etc.). The largest class of arthropods—and indeed the largest class in the animal kingdom—is that of the insects, to which butterflies belong.

All insects have certain things in common: a head, thorax, abdomen, six legs, and one pair of antennae. Lepidoptera is a very distinctive order of insects, second only to Coleoptera (beetles) in the number of species. It is difficult to determine exactly how many species of lepidopterans there are since many new ones are described every year. Many more are certain to be discovered in the future, adding to the 150,000 or so already known. Butterflies, including recently extinct forms, account for about 25,000 of these species.

Many people think of butterflies and moths as though they were two equivalent subdivisions of Lepidoptera, but the division into "butterflies" and "moths" has little scientific validity, though it is still used for convenience. Conventionally, butterflies have clubbed antennae, fly by day, and are often brightly colored; whereas moths are nocturnal, usually dull colored, and have tapered or feathery antennae. The looseness of such a classification is shown by the abundance of exceptions—for example, the many colorful day-flying moths (such as the spectacular Hummingbird Clearwing Moth) some of which even have clubbed antennae.

An alternative distinction is based upon the way in which the wings are linked during flight. In moths there is usually a lobe in the forewing or spines on the hindwing that act as a coupling mechanism. In butterflies the coupling is achieved by the large area of overlap of the fore and hind wings, but this is again subject to exceptions.

Left: The distinctions between moths and butterflies frequently become blurred, as evidenced by the spectacular hummingbird clearwing moth (*Hemaris thysbe*). This moth adds to the confusion by emulating a hummingbird.

Above: The evolution of butterflies over the millennia has produced some amazing environmental adaptations. This yellow angled-sulphur (*Anteos maerula*) butterfly, photographed in the Butterfly Rainforest in Gainesville, Florida, shows that it's not necessarily the survival of the fittest that counts but the survival of the most deceptive.

The Butterfly Body

Adult butterflies are built on the same general plan as their other insect relatives such as wasps, bees, and beetles. The body is protected by an armor of chitin (forming the exoskeleton), which is arranged in a series of rings or segments separated by flexible membranous zones that allow movement to take place. The body consists of three main regions—the head, the thorax, and the abdomen—all with a specialized structure to equip them for different functions in the life of the insect. Each part is covered in a layer of minute scales that are responsible for the soft, downy appearance of the body as well as the frequently vivid coloration so characteristic of butterflies.

The Head

The head is a small spherical capsule that bears the feeding apparatus and sensory structures. Many adult butterflies feed on nectar from flowers, although honeydew (the sweet secretion produced by aphids), decaying fruit, the sap exuding from damaged trees, excrement, or the juices of carrion are examples of other butterfly foods. The harvester butterfly is exceptional in North America in that it is carnivorous.

Butterfly adults have no jaws and must always take their food in liquid form using a specially modified "tongue" or proboscis. This is a long, hollow tube, which is coiled like a watchspring and tucked under the

Opposite: A harvester butterfly (*Feniseca tarquinius*) stops to drink water along the Tellico River near Tallassee, Tennessee. The harvester has the unique distinction of having the only carnivorous caterpillar in North America.

Below: The butterfly head and thorax.

19

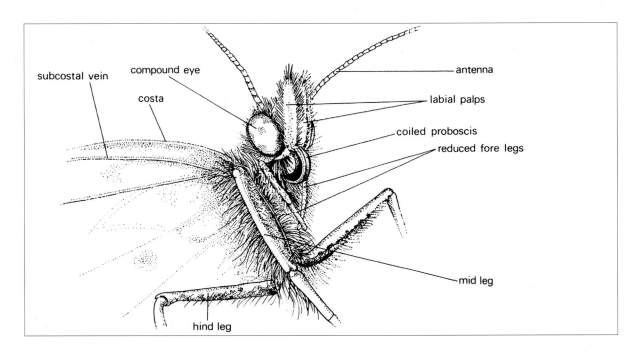

subcostal vein

compound eye

costa

antenna

labial palps

coiled proboscis

reduced fore legs

mid leg

hind leg

Above: Face-to-face with a skipper butterfly (*Hesperiidae*), showing some extraordinary detail on the club-ended antennae. Butterflies use these organs for balance and, most importantly, smell.

head when not in use. Through an increase in blood pressure, it can be quickly unrolled to probe deep into flowers. This feeding tube is composed of two parts that are grooved on their inner surface and joined along their length by tiny interlocking spines. The liquid food is sucked up the central channel between the two parts, and there is a special type of pump in the head to assist in this.

Since butterflies never bite or chew their food, jaws or mandibles are absent. Instead, they have a pair of sensory palps, or feelers (labial palps), one on each side of the proboscis. These palps are covered with scales and sensory hairs, and serve to test the suitability of the food source.

The antennae are typically club-ended in butterflies. Each antenna consists of a series of rings or segments, and both the number of segments and size of the club varies in different families; the skippers (*Hesperiidae*), for example, often have very pronounced "hooks." The antennae are sense organs that are responsible for balance and smell. The base of the antenna houses a specialized collection of sensory cells, called the Johnston's organ, which is crucial in sensing the insect's orientation, particularly during flight. The smell receptors are scattered over the entire surface of the antenna.

The eyes of butterflies are conspicuous hemispherical swellings on the top of the head. They are called "compound" eyes because each eye is composed of a large number of optical units, or ommatidia. The individual ommatidium resembles a simple eye with a lens and a light receptive region, and each one is capable of forming its own visual image. Each ommatidium is sheathed by a layer of pigment that serves to separate it from its neighbors. A butterfly therefore sees its surroundings as a complex mosaic of tiny pictures, each picture being created by a single ommatidium. Although butterflies can readily detect the movement of objects, the acuity of their vision is much inferior to that of humans. They are able to detect a limited number of different colors by discriminating between light sources of different wavelengths. This simple color vision may be illustrated by the fact that certain types of butterflies will frequent flowers of a particular color; for example, swallowtails (*Papilionidae*) regularly visit red flowers. Butterflies are also capable of detecting ultraviolet light, which is invisible to humans, and this suggests they may well see the color of flowers in quite a different way than we do.

Above: Swallowtails, such as this black swallowtail (*Papilio polyxenes*) are particularly drawn to red flowers. In this instance, though, a recently emerged male, photographed in Minnesota, is drying its wings on a cardinal flower before taking flight.

The Thorax

The middle zone, or thorax, of the body is the locomotory region, where both the legs and wings are located. The head is joined to the thorax by a flexible neck, or cervix. The thorax is composed of three segments, and each carries a pair of legs adapted for both walking and clinging. Each leg consists of several regions: the basal joint (coxa), the thigh (femur), the shank (tibia), and the foot (tarsus). The coxa and femur are joined by a small triangular segment, the trochanter. The foot commonly has five joints and ends in a pair of claws. In brushfoots (*Nymphalidae*), the front legs are very short and held close to the body, giving the odd appearance of an insect with only four legs.

Right: An example of reduced front legs, typical of the brushfoot butterflies. This painted lady (*Vanessa cardui*) has two pairs of sturdy legs to perch on, while the front pair—visible as dark brown lines below the eyes—are not so well defined. These reduced legs are used to taste adult food and larval host plant sources.

Surprisingly, butterflies also use their feet to taste their food, so there are numerous sense organs on their tarsi.

The two pairs of wings belong to the second and third thoracic segments (meso- and metathorax). The delicate wings consist of an upper and lower membrane with a framework of hollow tubes between the layers. These supporting tubes are called veins, and they are arranged in a very precise way. The overall pattern, or venation, is often a diagnostic feature of a group of butterflies, and consequently wing venation is an important tool in classification. The principal veins are given names according to their position on the wing.

At the base of the wings are some small structures known as sclerites that form a flexible articulation between the wings and the thorax. These

Below: Butterflies can use their feet to taste. Here a Marius hairstreak (*Rekoa marius*) investigates a flower part in Palmview South, Texas.

23

permit the beating of the wings in flight and also allow them to be folded away when at rest, in the upright position, characteristic of butterflies. During flight the movements of the two wings on each side are coupled or linked together in a special way. Usually the hind wing has a lobe that presses against the forewing, thus ensuring that wing movements are synchronized to give maximum efficiency.

Butterflies are typically active during the day (diurnal), and most species fly only in bright sunshine. The height at which they fly varies; some merely skim across the surface of low vegetation while others fly much higher.

The color patterns on the wings are due to the covering of scales. The scales overlap each other in a regular fashion, resembling

Above and left: Close-ups of butterfly wings showing the individual pigment scales that give species their identity and allow butterfly enthusiasts to distinguish between male and female (in most species). Butterflies rely more on smell to identify potential mates.

tiles on a roof. Each scale is more or less racket-shaped and has a small projection, or stalk, at its base that fits into a tiny socket on the wing membrane. To the naked eye, the scales look like colored dust. Pigments contained within the scales give rise to the color of some butterflies, while in others, microscopic ridges, or striae, on the surface break up the light falling on them and so produce the metallic colors of the blues and coppers.

Scattered among the scales are specialized scent scales known as androconia, which are peculiar to the males. At the base of these scales is a small gland that produces an aphrodisiac to excite the female during courtship. The volatile secretion passes up the hollow stalk of the scale and is disseminated by the fine hairlike processes, or plumes, at its tip. During courtship, the male often flutters around the female waving his wings and attempting to stimulate her by his scent.

Below: A male spicebush swallowtail (*Papilio troilus*) tries to impress a female (on the right) with his scent at the Scherman Hoffman Wildlife Sanctuary in Bernardsville, New Jersey.

25

Above: Common blue butterflies (*Polyommatus icarus*) mating on tansy flowers. The female (on the right) has more pallid coloring than the male, though both have the same markings underneath.

The Abdomen

The abdomen is much softer than the head and thorax and consists of ten rings or segments, of which only seven or eight can easily be seen. The end segments are specialized for reproductive purposes and are generally known as tile genitalia. In the male there is a pair of claspers that grip the female during mating and surround the central ejaculatory organ. The presence of a pair of claspers at the hind end of the body is a simple and reliable way to distinguish the sexes. In the female, some fusion of the terminal segments occurs to give rise to an egg-laying tube, or ovipositor. The ovipositor is normally telescoped inside the body of the female. There is a special separate opening that receives the sperm from the male.

Once ready for mating, the female settles and the male grasps the end of her abdomen with his claspers. Pairing takes some time, and the two insects may remain together for an hour or so. The male passes his sperm to the female in a package called a spermatophore, which she retains inside her body until egg laying begins. If the couple is disturbed during pairing, they will take to flight with one partner being dominant and dragging the other after it. A male is capable of mating with several females.

Internal Structures

Within the toughened exoskeleton of an insect, the internal organs are bathed in blood. Unlike humans, the blood system does not consist of veins and arteries but instead the whole of the body cavity is one large, blood-filled space (the hemocoel). Circulation of the blood is maintained by a long, tubular heart that lies along the back (dorsal surface) of the insect. The heart has muscular walls that contract rhythmically and push the blood, or hemolymph, forward into the blood space. On its return from the body tissues, the blood reenters the heart via small pores, or ostia.

Digestion

The digestive system is specially designed to cope with a liquid diet. The base of the "tongue," or proboscis, opens into a spherical muscular region, the pharynx. This region is often referred to as a "sucking pump," since it is responsible for drawing liquids up the long proboscis. The sucking action is brought about quite simply by a change in volume of the pharynx. The enlargement of the pharynx creates within it a partial vacuum, and the liquid in the proboscis is drawn upward and into the pharynx. The muscular walls then contract, and this serves to push the meal into the esophagus, which is the next region of the alimentary canal. Once inside the digestive tract, the food may be stored in a small reservoir, or crop, until it is needed. The actual digestion of the food takes place in the stomach, and any unsuitable material is passed into the hindgut and is voided as feces, via the anus. The digested food is absorbed into the blood and is stored as fat in a structure known as the fat body until it is needed. The fat body takes the form of sheets of fatty tissue, which either underlie the outer integument (membrane) of the insect or surround the digestive tract. The fat body is usually better

28

Above: Close-up of a butterfly's neatly curled proboscis. Its lack of mandibles means that it can take in nutrients only in a liquid form, but they are not limited to nectar. Some feed on honeydew, and red admirals (*Vanessa atalanta*) sometimes feed on rotting apples.

developed in the female since it is also needed to provide nourishment for her developing eggs.

Excretion is performed by structures known as Malpighian tubules. In their mode of functioning they closely resemble kidneys, although in appearance they are very different. The tubules are long filaments attached to the alimentary canal at the beginning of the hindgut. They float freely in the hemocoel and extract waste products from the circulating blood. These substances (collectively referred to as urine) are passed through the tubules and into the hindgut; from here they leave the body with the feces.

Above: A fritillary butterfly (*Speyeria*), photographed during the summertime in Duluth, Minnesota, exhibits just how far it can stick out its proboscis.

Left: Here's what most butterflies are hoping to end up with: a proboscis filled with nectar.

Nerve Centers

The nervous system is composed of nerve cells, or neurons, which are grouped together in nerve centers, or ganglia. One of these is situated in the head and is generally referred to as the brain. The brain is connected to a nerve cord that lies under the digestive tract and passes to the hind end of the body. The nerve cord has a number of subsidiary ganglia along its length. Most butterflies have two ganglia in the thorax and four in the abdomen. From these centers, smaller nerves pass to all parts of the body. Special nerve cells (visceral nerves) are associated with the digestive system and reproductive system while others (peripheral nerves) innervate the surface of the body.

Reproduction

The internal reproductive organs of insects consist of a pair of gonads and a system of tubes, or ducts, to carry their products (either sperm or eggs) to the outside of the body. In the female, each ovary consists of four egg tubes, or ovarioles. Each contains a large number of eggs at various stages of development. There is a special saclike storage chamber (bursa) that retains the sperm until the eggs are ripe and about to be laid; only then are they fertilized. The female also has accessory glands associated with the reproductive system that secrete a sticky substance used for cementing her eggs to the substrate on which they are laid. The male has a pair of testes, which are fused together in some butterflies. Sperm reservoirs are also present, which store the sperm prior to pairing.

Above: A lacewing butterfly (*Cethosia*) carefully laying eggs along a plant stem. Females will choose only host plants that their larvae will eat. If eggs are laid on the wrong plant, the caterpillars will sometimes die of starvation rather than eat an alien plant.

Oxygen Limits

In many animals, including humans, oxygen is carried around the body by the blood, but in butterflies and other insects, the organs of the body are separately supplied with oxygen by a system of "air tubes," or tracheae. These open to the atmosphere through special apertures in the exoskeleton called spiracles, of which there are nine pairs in butterflies. The actual exchange of gases takes place by simple diffusion at the ends of the tracheae, where the tubes become very narrow. In active insects the diffusion of oxygen into the body and the passage of carbon dioxide out is speeded up by ventilatory actions of the body, comparable with our own breathing movements. Even so, the system is relatively inefficient and the amount of oxygen available to the insect is quite small. This crucial point represents one of the main limitations on the size of butterflies, and without a major redesign of their whole system they cannot ever be more than relatively small creatures.

Below: To give an indication of scale, a tiny harvester (*Feniseca tarquinius*) rests on a forefinger. Small butterflies have no problem distributing oxygen around their body, but they use a relatively inefficient system, which limits the size to which they can grow.

The Butterfly Life Cycle

Butterflies are examples of endopterygotes: insects that will characteristically undergo a complete change, or metamorphosis, during the course of their development. Their life cycle includes both a larval and a pupal stage before the adult insect, or imago, emerges. The larva, or caterpillar, is completely different from the adult, both in appearance and habits. The pupa is an inactive, nonfeeding stage that gives rise to the adult. In grasshoppers, which are an example of an exopterygote, development is much more gradual with a series of young stages, or nymphs, that all resemble the adult and become progressively more like it at each successive stage. In these insects, there is no pupal stage.

Right: The eggs of the owl butterfly (*Caligo memnon*), which is found in Mexico. Butterfly eggs can be hardy, and many species produce eggs intended for overwintering.

Opposite: Like tiny corn husks, these are eggs of the gulf fritillary (*Agraulis vanillae*). In the wild, the adult females will seek out passion vines on which to lay their eggs.

34

The Egg

Female butterflies usually lay their eggs on or very near the food plant on which the larva feeds. The site is carefully chosen, and touch, smell, taste, and sight are probably all involved in its selection. Most species lay their eggs singly and cement them to the plant by a sticky secretion. The eggs are usually laid on a particular part of the plant— for example, on the leaves, flower heads, or in crevices in the bark. Most frequently, they are laid on the underside of the leaf; the female alights on the upper surface and curves her abdomen under the leaf until a suitable position is found. Here the eggs are protected from rain and sunshine, and to some extent from predators. However, a large number of eggs are laid by a single female to ensure that at least some will hatch successfully. The large white (*Pieris brassicae*) often lays clusters of a hundred or more eggs, while a few others lay smaller batches of five to fifteen eggs. The arrangement of the eggs varies; they may form regular bands around twigs or pendant strings of eggs. A small number of species merely scatter their eggs at random as they fly over vegetation, usually grassland.

35

Butterfly eggs are commonly yellow or green in color, although they usually darken just before hatching. The shape of the egg varies in different species and may be spherical or oval and flattened. The shell is often elaborately sculptured with regular ribs or pits (reticulations). At the top of the egg is a slight depression within which is a minute opening or micropyle. The micropyle marks the entry point of the male sperm into the egg, and once the egg is laid, air and moisture pass to the developing embryo through this pore. Food is contained inside the egg in the form of yolk, which is gradually consumed as the young larva develops.

Just before hatching, the fully formed embryo can be seen curled up within the transparent eggshell, or chorion. The young larva gnaws its way through the shell, and after hatching may continue to eat the shell until only the base is left.

In the case of the large white butterfly (*Pieris brassicae*), which lays its eggs in clusters, a newly hatched larva may also eat off the tops of other unhatched eggs. The shell contains valuable nutrients and is immediately available to the larva. After the shell, the food plant on which the egg was laid will be devoured.

Above and opposite: A monarch butterfly (*Danaus plexippus*) caterpillar emerges from its egg—laid on the leaf of a common milkweed plant—and begins life by eating its eggshell. Subsequent feeding on the leaf will concentrate poisons from the plant within its body. This renders the growing caterpillar toxic and therefore distasteful to predators.

The Larva

Butterfly larvae, or caterpillars as they are better known, are variable in color and in shape, although their basic structure is relatively constant. The larva has a head followed by thirteen trunk segments, of which the first three are regarded as the thorax and the remainder, the abdomen. The larval skin, or cuticle, is soft and flexible, though spines or bristles (setae), which arise from surface tubercles, may be present. These are particularly characteristic of the brushfoot family (*Nymphalidae*).

The head is a hardened round capsule with a completely different array of structures than the adult butterfly. The larvae feed on plant material that is relatively tough to a small insect. Consequently, the mouthparts are modified for biting and chewing. There is a prominent

Below: A more developed form of the monarch caterpillar—at the fourth instar phase—photographed in Raleigh, North Carolina. Colorful caterpillars advertise to potential predators that they are posionous.

36

pair of toothed jaws, or mandibles, which bite off fragments of food and shred them into fine pieces. The maxillae, which form the proboscis in the adult, are very small and are used to guide the food into the mouth. The other main mouthpart (the labium) is modified to form the spinneret, which is used in silk production.

Compound eyes are lacking, the main visual organs being the lateral ocelli. These are arranged in two groups of six, one group on either side of the head. The ocelli in many ways resemble the single optical unit, or ommatidium, of the adult's compound eye. Each ocellus has a lens and receptive part, or retina. It seems that they are unable to create an image of their visual field and probably only detect the difference between dark and light. The head also bears a pair of short, stubby antennae.

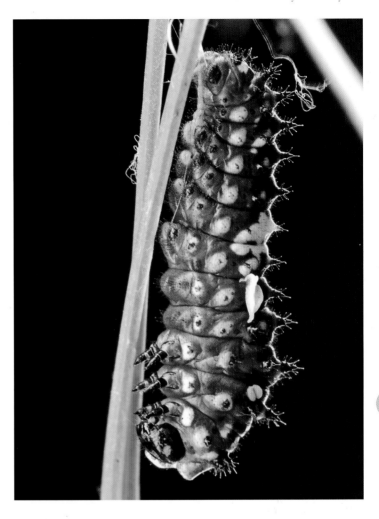

37

Above: A black swallowtail caterpillar (*Papilio polyxenes*) navigating its way down a wild parsley stem in McLean County, Illinois.

Left: Fully armored and expecting trouble, the caterpillar of the comma butterfly (*Polygonia c-album*) seeks additional food along a red currant stem.

38

Above: The striking, red-colored caterpillar of the variegated fritillary butterfly (*Euptoieta claudia*), seen here in a garden in Mars Hill, North Carolina.

The three segments of the thorax each have a pair of short, jointed legs, or prolegs, that end in a single claw. A final pair on the last segment are called claspers, and some larvae will be torn in half rather than release their hold with them. The end of each proleg is flattened and has a series of hooks, or crochets, that help the larva in locomotion. When not being used, the prolegs can be withdrawn into the body.

Since the skin of the larva is soft, it does not provide a suitable skeleton for the attachment of muscles, as the exoskeleton does in the adult. Consequently, the body has to be kept turgid by the pressure of the body fluid (hemolymph)—much like an earthworm. The characteristic crawling movement consists of a coordinated interaction between the muscles of the body wall and the internal pressure of the hemolymph.

As the larvae grow, they entirely fill their skin, which becomes very tight. In order for further growth to occur, this skin is shed from time to time, exposing a new and larger one that has formed beneath it. Rapid expansion of the "new" larva occurs before the skin becomes toughened. This shedding of the skin is known as molting, or ecdysis, and usually takes place four or five times before the larva is fully grown. Each growth stage between molts is known as an instar. An insect's molting is carefully and precisely controlled by hormones, although environmental conditions and the availability of food may cause variations in the duration of the instars.

Food Sources

The larvae feed mainly on the leaves of flowering plants and trees. While some butterfly caterpillars feed on a variety of plants types, larvae are usually extraordinarily specific in their feeding habits and will feed only on a small number of closely related plant species. If a suitable food plant is not available, then larvae will starve to death rather than eat something else. A larva recognizes its food plants by certain aromatic

Below: Caterpillars of the brushfoot family (here a fritillary) rely heavily on spines for their defense.

39

Right: The mandibles of a
well-developed caterpillar in
close-up. Note the false eyespot
above the head. Their limited
vision is provided by means
of six pairs of ocelli, or simple
eyes, on either side of the
mandibles. In this photo,
only four are prominent.

40

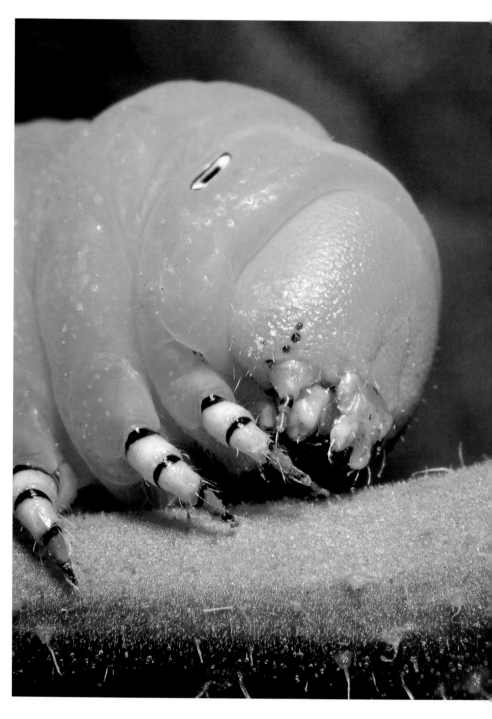

vegetable oils that they contain. It is generally thought that selection may
depend upon the detection of chemical attractants in the food species
and of repellents in other plants.

The larva is the main feeding stage in the life cycle, and when they
are present in sufficient numbers, caterpillars can defoliate large areas of

vegetation. The way in which a larva tackles a leaf is often characteristic of the species; some eat holes in the leaf, while others attack the leaf margin. In some species, feeding occurs at night and in others by day. Generally, periods of active feeding alternate with periods of rest. Feeding ceases a day or so before a molt, but resumes as soon as the new skin is fully developed.

The droppings of the larvae are discrete, oval structures and are referred to as frass. Since much of the plant material consists of indigestible cellulose, a large amount of frass is produced and may even form a distinct layer under small trees or shrubs on which many larvae have been feeding.

41

Above: Seconds after it has molted, a black swallowtail caterpillar (*Papilio polyxenes*) steps out of its old skin and continues up the stem of this dill plant.

The Pupa

The end of larval life is marked by another molt, which gives rise to a pupa, or chrysalis. Fully grown larvae often select special sites to undergo this transformation and may, for example, leave their food plant and enter the soil. The digestive tract is emptied and the larval skin

shrivels and eventually splits to expose the pupa. During the pupal period, much of the larval tissue is remolded to give rise to adult structures, particularly the wings, mouthparts, and reproductive organs.

The pupa is immobile and neither eats nor drinks, since the mouth and anus are sealed over. The only functional openings in the pupal case are the spiracles, which permit the exchange of respiratory gases. The legs and antennae are firmly stuck down and cannot be moved. Externally, the pupa usually appears brown or green. All the major features of the adult can be seen if one looks closely within the pupal skin, but one specialized structure is to be found at the end of the abdomen, where a number of hooks form the cremaster. This is used for the attachment of the pupa to the substrate, such as a twig or branch.

It is often desirable to distinguish the sex of a pupa before the adult emerges, and this is not usually difficult. In the male there is a single genital opening on the ninth abdominal segment, while in the female there are two such openings, one on the eighth and another on the ninth segment of the abdomen.

Since the pupa is immobile, it is particularly vulnerable to attack by predators—and pupation occasionally proceeds within a silken cocoon. This may take the form of a hollow of earth lined with silk, or a roll of leaves fastened together with silk threads (as in the case of many of the skippers). Silk cocoons are generally much better developed among moths. In some butterflies the pupa is naked, but it is then usually protectively colored. The naked pupa may hang upside down, attached only by the cremaster.

Above: Even encased within its pupal case, it is possible to identify that this is a monarch (*Danaus plexippus*), close to the end of its period of metamorphosis—day nine, to be exact.

42

Above and left: The process of an adult butterfly emerging from its pupal case is known as "eclosion." Here, a clouded yellow butterfly ecloses into the world. The process is often so rapid that photographers miss the key moment. In this case, the photographer's patience and fast shutter reaction were rewarded.

43

The Adult

The emergence of the adult, or imago, is preceded by the color pigment appearing in the wing scales. The wing patterns of the adult can be seen through the pupal case. The skin of the pupa splits behind the head; the insect first frees its legs and antennae and after a short while withdraws the rest of its body. Those species pupating within a cocoon have to free themselves from this as well as the pupal skin. Immediately after emergence, the wings are soft and crumpled. The butterfly moves to a place from where its wings can hang downward and blood is forced into them. The wings expand by the flattening of the numerous tiny folds and soon become the typical thin sheets supported by hollow veins. Once they have reached their full size, the insect holds them apart until they are completely dry and hardened. The excretory material, which has accumulated in the closed digestive tract during the pupal period, is ejected from the anus.

Interruption of the Life Cycle

The duration of the life cycle varies in different species. Some may have a single, complete generation in a year while others have two or even more. Unfavorable climatic conditions such as a cold winter in temperate regions or a dry season in the tropics often necessitate an interruption in the life cycle. Any of the developmental stages—egg, larva, or pupa—may enter a period of arrested development, or diapause. This delay in development is induced by environmental conditions such as day length, but cannot then be terminated until a predetermined period has passed. This ensures that the insects do not emerge too early during temporary favorable periods only to be caught out by a resumption of harsh conditions. The eggs and pupae are protected by their outer eggshell or pupae skins, respectively, while the overwintering larvae usually shelter at the base of their food plant or in a specially produced larval cocoon formed from plant leaves and silk.

Climatic Factors

Daily fluctuations in temperature and moisture are important to insects, and when they are subjected to extremes, heavy mortality may result. Butterflies, like reptiles, are cold-blooded animals and have to derive their body heat from external sources. They warm up by basking in the sun, usually with the wings outspread and the body oriented so that the maximum area of the wings is exposed to the sun. The color patterns on the wings may assist in heat absorption; those species with large black patches are particularly efficient at absorbing heat. Butterflies cool themselves by seeking the shade, or if shelter is not available they may close their wings together and face the sun so that the smallest possible surface is exposed to the sun's rays. Excessive dryness is avoided by the larvae or adults seeking out areas of high humidity for resting sites. Adult butterflies shelter from heavy rain by settling on the underside of leaves with their wings held slightly open so that the rain

Below: A red-spotted purple (*Limenitis arthemis*) basks in the October sun on the Greenbrier River Trail in West Virginia.

Above: Butterflies regulate their temperature by opening and closing their wings. This painted lady (*Vanessa cardui*) is minimizing its surface exposure to the sun while feeding on the nectar of a blossom.

can run off them. If the wings were held tightly together in their usual resting posture, and then became wet, the surface layer of scales might become damaged. Generally, butterflies are not found flying in high winds, although during the migration flights of some species they are able to look after themselves satisfactorily. Other phenomena, such as forest fires, may have a serious effect on a butterfly population; the adults are usually able to fly to another suitable area, but their eggs, larvae, and pupae risk total destruction.

Below: A clouded sulphur (*Colias philodice*) takes shelter under a leaf during rainfall, but still can't avoid getting a drop on the end of its antenna.

Methods of Self-defense

All stages of the life cycle are vulnerable to attack by predators, which may include other insects as well as spiders, reptiles, and small mammals. Consequently, butterflies have evolved methods of protection that reduce the chance of attack by these predators. There are two main types of protection: those that enable the butterfly to escape attention because of its close resemblance to the surroundings and those that make the butterfly appear startling and unattractive—an indication that it is unpalatable to the predator.

Generally, the eggs of butterflies are laid on the underside of a leaf and are relatively small, so they are unlikely to be noticed. However, the inactive, soft-bodied larvae are very prone to attack, and it is this stage in the life cycle that displays a wide range of these protective devices. Some larvae spin silken webs and live in groups within them. Many larvae are colored to blend with their surroundings, while in the young stages of the white admiral (*Limenitis arthemis*), camouflage is taken

Below: An older caterpillar of the white admiral butterfly (*Limenitis arthemis*), here resembling something that a bird deposited. In its earlier forms it is known to cover itself with its own waste, or frass.

48

Left: A perfect example of blending into the surroundings as a means of defense. While many caterpillars emulate bird droppings or twigs, and adult leafwing butterflies can resemble fallen brown leaves or living green ones, this moth caterpillar blends effortlessly into the bark of a birch tree.

50

Above: A black swallowtail caterpillar displaying its bright orange osmeterium—like a pair of fleshy antennae—on its head. When alarmed, the caterpillar will use this organ to exude a noxious smell to deter any would-be predator.

a stage further by the larvae adorning themselves with their own frass. The later stages do not adopt this habit and rely solely on protective coloration. Another difference in the protective devices employed by young and more mature larvae is seen in the swallowtail, where the very young instars are dark and resemble bird droppings, while the later instars are brightly colored.

Several types of warning devices are found in the larvae of butterflies. The brushfoots (*Nymphalidae*) are often brightly colored and have an armor of sharp spines. Other larvae may produce an obnoxious smell or have an unpleasant taste. Swallowtails (*Papilionidae*) have a gland just behind the head called the osmeterium that produces a strong odor when the larvae are disturbed. In other families, similar defensive glands may be present on other parts of the body. Some gregarious larvae may jerk their bodies in unison to deter predators. Occasionally a palatable larva may copy or mimic a distasteful one and avoid predation this way.

The pupae are usually protected by their cryptic coloration patterns and sometimes their shape. For example, the pupa of the orange tip (*Anthocharis cardamines*) closely resembles a plant bud. The pupae of some brushfoots may be spiny, rather like the larvae. Larvae normally seek out safe sites for pupation and consequently the pupae are found in inconspicuous positions, and some occur within cocoons formed from dried leaves or are hidden in the ground.

The adult butterfly is most vulnerable immediately after its emergence from the pupa, before the wings have expanded and dried. After this, the insect can take to flight and avoid many predators. Most species visit flowers to suck nectar and are frequently attacked when they alight on the flower. Protective coloration is also employed by adult butterflies whose wings may have a brilliantly colored upper surface but are cryptically colored below so that when they are folded together at rest the insect completely harmonizes with its surroundings.

Some families have eyespots on the edges of their wings, especially satyrs, and some may also have long tails to their wings. Both the eyespots and the tails are thought to attract the attention of predators, and by attacking these parts the actual body of the butterfly is left undamaged. Some species, such as the monarch (*Danaus plexippus*), produce an obnoxious odor.

Above: This little wood satyr (*Megisto cymela*), with its wings folded, reveals multiple eyespots. It was photographed at the Detroit River Wildlife Refuge.

51

Left: Looking like a plant spur or bud, the pupal case of an orange tip butterfly (*Anthocharis cardamines*) hangs onto a plant stem by a slender silken thread.

The Role of Parasites

Parasites are creatures that live either on or within the body of another animal, the host. Butterflies, particularly their larvae, are especially prone to attack by parasites, many of which are very highly adapted both in their structure and in their own life cycles to take advantage of them.

Often, among animals, the parasite's way of life is carefully balanced so that both the host and parasite survive. However, in the case of an attack by these insect parasites, the host usually dies. In this sense the parasites almost resemble predators, and they are then usually described as parasitoids.

A typical parasitoid lays her eggs in the larvae, or occasionally on the eggs or pupae, first piercing the host's skin with her sharp ovipostor. Then, a large number of eggs are laid in each host. The eggs hatch and feed on the internal tissues of the host, initially consuming the fat body and later attacking the more vital organs such as the digestive tract and nervous system. This internal destruction results in the death of the host before it has completed pupation. The fully fed parasite larvae then eat their way out of the host and pupate on or near the carcass in bright yellow cocoons from which the adult parasites eventually emerge.

Opposite: The caterpillar of this silvery blue butterfly (*Glaucopsyche lygdamus*) has a "honey gland," which secretes a substance attractive to ants. The ants feed on the substance and tend the caterpillar, protecting it from predators in a symbiotic relationship.

Below: Like a scene from a horror movie, this moth caterpillar has been devoured by parasitic wasp larvae. After they have disposed of their host, they form their own cocoons around the body and pupate.

52

Right: Ants busy attending to a caterpillar of the hairstreak family. Many butterflies are locked in symbiotic relationships with ants, and the absence of ants can result in the butteflies dying out. In some species, adult females seek out ant nests, on which they lay their eggs.

54

Other parasites live on the outside of their host, where they suck the body fluids. Mites are examples of these ectoparasites and are found associated with butterflies from time to time. Mortality is also caused by bacterial and fungal diseases that are particularly prevalent in conditions of high humidity. Considerable care has to be exercised in rearing butterflies in captivity to prevent diseases caused by these organisms, since they normally result in the death of the entire colony.

Ants That Serve

An association between butterflies and other insects is not always harmful. An example of one that is mutually beneficial is the relationship between ants and many species of blues and coppers (*Lycaenidae*). The larvae of these butterflies have a honey gland that exudes small droplets of a sweet fluid. This is extremely attractive to ants, which "attend" the larvae and stimulate the production of the fluid by stroking movements of the legs and antennae. The ants are pugnacious insects and serve as a deterrent to the usual predators and parasites of the butterfly larvae. The ants never damage the larvae, but merely lick the gland, enjoying the secretion it produces. Some larvae are dependent on the ants, and their development is impaired if the ants are absent.

Butterfly Mobility

On the whole, insects living in permanent habitats, such as established woodland, tend to migrate less than species in temporary habitats, such as fields of agricultural crops. Even permanent habitats may be temporary for a given species, because either the weather is suitable only at certain times of the year, or its food plant is available only in certain seasons. In order for any insect species to survive in habitats that are temporary, it must develop either a resistant resting stage in the life cycle or be able to move out of the habitat before conditions become unfavorable, and then migrate back again when conditions are favorable.

The movement of whole populations of butterflies from place to place in the form of mass flights provides one of the most spectacular examples of insect migration. These migrations often take the form of persistent flights in one direction over a long distance by large numbers of butterflies. Anyone who has witnessed the mass migrations of the painted lady (*Vanessa cardui*) from the Mexico-California border northward will have been struck by the vast numbers of insects moving purposefully as if guided by a compass. However, this butterfly does not establish itself permanently after the migration, and there is no return flight.

Right: A painted lady (*Vanessa cardui*), too busy basking in the sun to contemplate migration.

Above: A great southern white (*Ascia monuste*) captured in flight at some distance from the Florida coast, in Mission, Texas.

Why Do Butterflies Migrate?

Many theories have been put forward to explain what causes butterflies to migrate, and most of them center around the idea that migration occurs in response to unfavorable conditions, such as a lack of food.

A good example of a short-to-medium-range migrating butterfly is the great southern white (*Ascia monuste*). This butterfly breeds on the islands off the eastern coast of Florida, where there is a plentiful supply of its food plant, turtleweed (*Batis maritima*). The plant is a woody perennial and is common on coastal salt marshes. The butterfly breeds year-round in Florida but only for about four months in any one particular place, and at different times of the year according to latitude. Populations of butterflies tend to spread from the breeding site in one of two ways: they either diffuse slowly through the country as a result of daily movement in the form of short, random flights to find flowers on which to feed, or periodic mass migrations occur. The latter involve large populations at a time when food for the larvae is still abundant; the butterflies that join in one of these migrations are less than two days old and the females are sexually immature. The butterflies fly from the breeding site to their feeding site in the morning, as usual, and after feeding set off in large clouds along the coast, following the line of the shore or nearby roads. In calm weather they appear to be capable of controlling their direction; in windy conditions they may be blown off course somewhat, but some will fly in sheltered situations such as the leeward side of sand dunes. Some of these migrating butterflies have been followed for more than twelve miles, and some are known to have traveled eighty-one miles in one day, downwind. By no means do all the individuals cover the whole distance traveled by a group; many fall by the wayside and others lose their direction. Those that succeed find new breeding sites and revert to their normal nonmigratory activities of feeding, flying short distances, and laying eggs. The adults live for only about ten days, so any subsequent migration from the new breeding site will be done by subsequent generations.

The Migration of the Monarch

The supreme example of long-distance displacement among butterflies is the annual migration of the monarch (*Danaus plexippus*) in North America. The northern race of this beautiful insect migrates the length of the subcontinent, a distance of 2,000 miles between its breeding areas in Canada and the northern United States, and its overwintering sites in the southern United States, California, and Mexico.

Adult monarchs start to move south from the northern breeding sites in July, and by September vast numbers can be seen on the move. They typically move by daylight only, feeding on the way, and on the whole do not fly at a great height but maintain a southerly direction. Tagging of individual monarchs has proved beyond doubt that this butterfly regularly covers distances in excess of 1,180 miles in only a few days, and at average speeds of up to 80 miles per day. A distance of fifteen to twenty-two miles is a more typical day's flight. The longest recorded flight by an individual monarch is 3,000 miles. Opinions have differed

Below: The incredible and irrepressible monarch (*Danaus plexippus*) roosting in colonies on its way south.

57

as to how far most individuals fly and how much the migration is really made up of successive short migrations by different individuals. The tagging experiments emphasize the fact that individuals can cover great distances, as do sightings of monarchs several hundred miles out to sea and the occasional landings in Britain of these American butterflies, which have presumably strayed off course during their southerly flight.

Right: During spring and summer, the monarch leads a fairly solitary existance, but come fall they band together for their epic journey south. Once seen, this event is rarely forgotten.

At night and when the weather is poor, the butterflies roost in trees, often in large groups. Most of the movement occurs down the eastern United States and also on the West Coast, but migrations through mountain passes, several over 10,000 feet high, have been observed. There are many records that suggest that the insects are capable of directing their own flight, even in the face of a headwind of nine miles per hour. On the other hand, they are often seen being blown south by a strong north wind, which suggests that in the long run it is the wind direction and strength that determines where the migrating butterflies will end their journey.

Unlike the butterflies previously mentioned, some of the individual monarchs that complete the long journey south to overwinter make the hazardous return journey the following spring. But the flight back follows a completely different pattern. In late February and March, at the overwintering sites the monarchs court and mate before departing on their

return journey. As the butterflies fly north the females lay eggs on milkweeds that they encounter along the way. The returning individuals are only able to fly to the southern states and it is succeeding generations that eventually find their way back to the northern states and southern Canada.

Above: The monarch is believed to be the fastest of the migrating butterflies. Given that it must cover thousands of miles to avoid winter frosts, it needs to be swift.

Opposite: Captured in flight, this painted lady is already unfurling the proboscis as it stops for a nectar refill on a Michaelmas daisy.

The Speed of Flight

The remarkable distances covered by some migrating butterflies pose questions about the speed at which they fly, how long they can remain in the air, what sustains them in flight, and what makes them stay airborne for such a long time. Butterflies are not among the fastest-flying insects by any means: the painted lady (*Vanessa cardui*) has been observed flying at speeds of five to nine miles per hour, while one of the fastest known migrating butterflies is the monarch, which has been know to manage twenty miles per hour. To put this in perspective, some horseflies and honeybee workers can fly at speeds of up to forty miles per hour.

Flying for such long periods involves the use of enormous quantities of energy. This is provided from fat stored in the body, mainly in the abdomen in the form of a large mass of tissue called the fat body. Butterflies are well endowed with this fat body when they emerge; it makes up perhaps 30 percent of the total body weight after drying. After a long migration, this figure may be down as low as 1 percent in the case of the monarch, even though the insects will almost certainly have fed en route in order to partially replenish their energy reserves.

Swallowtails • *Papilionidae*
Anise Swallowtail

Papilio zelicaon • Wingspan: 2.8-3.5 inches (7-9 cm)

The anise swallowtail is a common swallowtail butterfly seen in all but the most arid spots of western North America. It can be seen patrolling hilltops or just as easily in the backyard.

Identification: The female is heavily marked in black and is larger than the male. There are black borders to the forewings in both sexes, black toward the base of the forewing, and a thick black border on the hind wing, dusted with blue. There are yellow marks on the forewing, an angled, underside hind wing with more blue dusting than the uppers, and eyespots on the hind wings.

Caterpillar: When newly hatched, the caterpillar is dark brown with an uneven white band across its middle. After a few days, the coloration changes and it becomes progressively more green at each successive molt until, in the fifth (and final) instar, it is predominantly green, with markings in black, orange, and light blue.

Caterpillar feeds on: Sweet fennel (anise), plants of the parsley family, and, rarely, cultivated citrus plants.

Similar species: There is the Old World swallowtail and a black form, similar to the black swallowtail, known as a "nitra."

Habitat: Various, from urban areas to forest clearings.

Mating flight: One in the north, year-round in California.

Distribution: From southwestern Canada and North Dakota in the north to Baja California in the South, and as far east as New Mexico.

Black Swallowtail

Papilio polyxenes • Wingspan: 3.2–4.3 inches (8–11 cm)

The black swallowtail is a common backyard butterfly that is widely distributed throughout the eastern part of the country, but doesn't make an appearance on the Pacific seaboard. It is also the state butterfly of Oklahoma.

Identification: A row of yellow spots and a yellow band across the wings, with orange-red eyespots; blue suffusion around the hind wings are more pronounced in females; orange background in east of range, yellow in the west.

Caterpillar: The black swallowtail caterpillar has an orange gland called the osmeterium. Around danger, the osmeterium, which looks like a snake's tongue, appears on top of its head.

Caterpillar feeds on: Plants of the parsley family, Queen Anne's lace, dill, fennel, and carrots.

Similar species: The Ozark swallowtail (*Papilio joanae*), which is limited to the Ozark mountain region. There is a subspecies, the desert black swallowtail (*Papilio polyxenes coloro*), which is found in southeastern California, southern Nevada, and western Arizona. It is smaller than the black swallowtail and may have a broader yellow band on the upper wing.

Habitat: Flowery open areas and gardens.

Mating flight: Three, from February to November.

Distribution: A large area stretching from Maine to Florida; east of the Great Lakes to the Dakotas; and south to New Mexico, Arizona, and southeastern California. Southern Manitoba, Ontario, and Maritimes.

Giant Swallowtail

Papilio cresphontes • Also known as orange dog swallowtail • Wingspan: 3.9–6.3 inches (10–16 cm)

The giant swallowtail is considered a pest to citrus farmers, but it can also be found in gardens where its larvae feed off ornamental citrus and related plants. Its flight is usually a series of strong flaps followed by glides at around head height that make it look like it is hopping through the air. It is the largest butterfly in the United States and Canada.

Identification: A large black butterfly with a yellow band across the uppers. Females are larger, with a series of yellow spots around the wings, and a yellow spot on the tail and toward the tip of the forewing. The underside is pale yellow throughout.

Caterpillar: The caterpillars resemble bird droppings as camouflage, and they have a red osmeterium that emits a smell deterrent. The later instars can take on the appearance of a small snake with head and eye markings.

Caterpillar feeds on: Citrus plant species, hence its alternative name, the orange dog swallowtail.

Habitat: Gardens, glades, roadsides, and citrus groves.

Mating flight: Year-round in Florida, from spring to fall farther north.

Distribution: Mostly East Coast from New York to Florida, west to the Mississippi, and occasionally even farther west to the Los Angeles basin. Common in southern Texas and resident in coastal southern California. Strays north to Colorado and the Great Plains.

Palamedes Swallowtail

Papilio Palamedes • Wingspan: 4.5–5.5 inches (11.5–14 cm)

This is a large, prominently marked swallowtail that is most at home in the swamplands of the Southeast.

Identification: A dart-shaped row of yellow spots crosses the forewings, repeated on the underside; hind wing underside with red darts in center and by the margin.

Caterpillar: The caterpillar is almost identical to the caterpillar of the spicebush swallowtail (*Papilio troilus*) except that it has smaller false eyes, larger blue spots, and is found on different host plants.

Caterpillar feeds on: Red bay, swamp bay, and white sassafras.

Habitat: Boggy, marshy areas and swampland.

Mating flight: February–December. Earliest and latest in the south.

Distribution: Southeastern United States, especially the Everglades, but ventures north up the eastern seaboard as far as southern New Jersey.

Pipevine Swallowtail

Battus philenor • Wingspan: 2.8–5.1 inches (7–13 cm)

The pipevine swallowtail is a large, striking butterfly often seen feeding on a range of flowers including thistles, lilac, bergamot, petunias, verbenas, and lupins.

Identification: The upper surface of the hind wings of the male butterfly have an iridescent metallic blue sheen. The hind wings also have a series of pale arrowhead markings above and a single row of seven round orange spots. The forewings are not as iridescent.

Caterpillar: The caterpillar is reddish brown, with prominent fleshy spikes along the length of the body.

Caterpillar feeds on: Pipevines, such as Virginia snakeroot.

Similar species: The pipevine swallowtail is mimicked by the black female eastern tiger swallowtail (*Papilio glaucus*), the spicebush swallowtail (*Papilio troilus*), the red-spotted purple (*Limenitis arthemis*), and the female Diana fritillary (*Speyeria diana*), which make use of the pipevine's unpalatable qualities to avoid predators.

Habitat: Fields, open woodland, and woodland margins.

Mating flight: In the East and in California, adults fly in late spring and summer. In the South and Southwest, it is more likely to be seen in late summer or fall.

Distribution: Principally southeastern United States, west to southern Arizona, and strays north to the Great Lakes and the Great Plains. A separate population is resident in central California.

Spicebush Swallowtail

Papilio troilus • Wingspan: 3–3.9 inches (7.5–10 cm)

The spicebush swallowtail makes use of its similarity to the pipevine to avoid predators, but it has the most distinctive of caterpillars. It is also the state butterfly of Mississippi.

Identification: Greenish-blue suffusion over most of the top surface of its hind wing; two rows of red spots on the underside of hind wing; forewings are dark with a row of yellow spots around the inside of margins.

Caterpillar: The caterpillars live in folded leaf shelters and eat leaves of the sassafras or spicebush. They bear eyespots that give them an almost cartoonlike character.

Caterpillar feeds on: Spicebush and sassafras trees, and also on prickly ash, tulip trees, and sweetbay.

Similar species: The spicebush swallowtail mimics the pipevine swallowtail, which is distasteful to predators.

Habitat: Woods, meadows, and forests.

Mating flight: April–October.

Distribution: East of the Mississippi and north to south Ontario and New Brunswick.

Eastern Tiger Swallowtail

Papilio glaucus • Also known as tiger swallowtail • Wingspan: 3.2–5.5 inches (8–14 cm)

A familiar large butterfly of the eastern states, it can often be seen gathered in large numbers on mud banks.

Identification: Yellow with black tiger stripes cross forewings and hind wings in both sexes; black tails, light underside with black highlighted veins; females are sometimes found as a black form, but both sexes have blue on the hind wings.

Caterpillar: Young caterpillars are brown and white and look like bird droppings. Older instars are green, with two black, yellow, and blue eyespots on the thorax.

Caterpillar feeds on: A variety of trees and shrubs, including cherry.

Similar species: The Canadian tiger swallowtail (*Papilio canadensis*) and the Appalachian tiger swallowtail (*Papilio appalachiensis*).

Habitat: Gardens, forests, and waysides.

Mating flight: March–November. Earliest and latest in the South.

Distribution: Most of North America, east of the Rockies, and as far as South Ontario.

Western Tiger Swallowtail

Papilio rutulus • Wingspan: 2.4–3.5 inches (6–9 cm)

A commonly sighted butterfly in the western part of the United States, often overlapping in range with the two-tailed swallowtail.

Identification: Similar to the eastern tiger swallowtail, but the yellow marginal band is continuous on the underside of the forewing.

Caterpillar: Resembles bird droppings and molts five times on its way to becoming bright green, with a pair of large yellow eyespots with black-and-blue pupils. They rest on silken mats in shelters of curled leaves.

Caterpillar feeds on: Leaves of cottonwood, cherry species, aspen, and willow.

Similar species: The eastern tiger swallowtail (*Papilio glaucus*) is very similar, but the western tiger has more prominent dark banding on wings.

Habitat: Near rivers and streams in woodland areas, including suburbs.

Mating flight: One, from June to July; two or more in lowland California.

Distribution: From the eastern slopes of the Rockies westward; from British Columbia in the northwest to California and Arizona in the southwest, though often only at altitude in Arizona.

75

Zebra Swallowtail

Eurytides marcellus • Wingspan: 2.4–3.5 inches (6–9 cm)

Has a distinctive black-and-white zebralike pattern to its wings. It is the only zebra swallowtail in the east and is the state butterfly of Tennessee. **Identification:** Long tails, though shorter in spring than in summer; triangular wings with double pairs of tiger marks crossing the white wings. Underside of hind wing shows a red median stripe. **Caterpillar:** Can be cannibalistic. Young instars are black; older instars are green with yellow and white lateral stripes. There is a rare black form that is black with white and orange lateral stripes. Possesses a defensive osmeterium.

Caterpillar feeds on: Pawpaw leaves.

Similar species: Pale swallowtail (*Papilio eurymedon*) found in the West from sea level to the timberline.

Habitat: Waysides, stream courses, and meadows.

Mating flight: March–December. Earliest and latest in the South.

Distribution: Southeastern United States; as far as New York in the north; occasionally southern Ontario.

Two-tailed Tiger Swallowtail

Papilio multicaudata • Wingspan: 3.5–5.1 inches (9–13 cm)

The largest of the western butterflies in North America, it bears a close resemblance to the giant swallowtail and the eastern and western tiger swallowtails. It is the state butterfly of Arizona.

Identification: Named after the two unequal tails on each hind wing; dark margins with yellow spots; centers of uppers are yellow with one black streak crossing the wings.

Caterpillar: The mature caterpillar is orange in color.

Caterpillar feeds on: The leaves of cherry, ash, and the hoptree.

Similar species: Apart from those mentioned above, there is a rare three-tailed tiger swallowtail (*Papilio pilumnus*) that strays into southern Texas.

Habitat: Gardens, damp canyons, creeks, and mountains.

Mating flight: February–November. Earliest and latest in the South.

Distribution: Western United States; southern British Columbia and southern Alberta in Canada.

Clodius Parnassian

Parnassius clodius • Wingspan: 2–2.4 inches (5–6 cm)

A large, slow-flying butterfly of California and the northwest.

Identification: Large, rounded wings, cream with a black-and-red spot in males; females have white-gray wings and a more dusty appearance on forewings, variable red spots on hind wings. The female develops a waxy pouch on her abdomen after mating.

Caterpillar: Black, covered with short black hairs and marked with a row of orange or yellow spots along the bottom of each side. Caterpillars feed at night near the base of the host plant and pupate in a silk cocoon.

Caterpillar feeds on: Plants in the bleeding heart family.

Habitat: Coasts, canyons, and mountains.

Mating flight: May–July.

Distribution: California, and from Utah north to British Columbia.

79

Whites and Sulphurs • *Pieridae*
Cabbage White

Pieris rapae • Also known as cabbage butterfly • Wingspan: 1.3–1.9 inches (3.2–4.7 cm)

One of the most common butterflies, introduced from Europe in the nineteenth century, it was originally known as the "imported cabbage worm" and is a pest of gardeners and farmers trying to grow *Brassica* crops.

Identification: The top side is creamy white with black tips to the forewings. Males have one black forewing spot, females have two; undersides are yellow or greenish.

Caterpillar: Green in color, not distasteful to predators, so they tend to occupy undersides of leaves.

Caterpillar feeds on: Plants of the *Brassica* species, such as cabbage, kale, and broccoli. Also watercress and mustard.

Habitat: Gardens, fields, roadsides, and meadows.

Mating flight: Several, from March to November.

Distribution: All of the contiguous United States and southern Canada, though less common in arid deserts and parts of Texas.

Checkered White

Pontia protodice • Also known as *Pieris protodice* • Wingspan: 1.4-2.3 inches (3.5-6.3 cm)

A common white butterfly with a rapid and erratic flight pattern.
Identification: Dark checkering over white forewing of females, which is more patterned than the male form. Spring forms and those from high altitudes are darker than summer and lowland individuals.

Caterpillar: Will eat buds, flowers, and fruits of its host plant as well as the leaves.

Caterpillar feeds on: Brassicas, including broccoli, turnips, brussels sprouts, and a variety of mustards.

Similar species: Western white.

Habitat: Wide variety, including roadsides, fields, and wastelands.

Mating flight: March–October. Earliest and latest in the South.

Distribution: Almost all of the contiguous United States and Mexico, as well as southern Canada, but more common in the South and West.

Pine White

Neophasia menapia • Wingspan: 1.8–2.3 inches (4.5–5.8 cm)

These are slow, high-flying white butterflies of the pine forests, only distantly related to other North American whites and observed in the tree canopy.

Identification: Male is white with black tips interrupted by white marks, also gray veins to hind wing. The female has a yellow background color, with margins of her hind wing tinged in orange.

Caterpillar: Caterpillars feed in groups when they are young, separating as they grow older. Caterpillars pupate at the base of the host tree.

Caterpillar feeds on: Needles of a variety of pines, especially Ponderosa pine and Douglas fir in California.

Similar species: Mexican pine white (*Neophasia terlooii*).

Habitat: Pine forests.

Mating flight: June–September.

Distribution: Pine forests in much of the western United States and southern British Columbia.

83

Western White

Pontia occidentalis • Wingspan: 1.5–2 inches (3.8–5.3 cm)

A widely distributed white butterfly that frequents uplands as far north as southwestern Canada.

Identification: Checkered to dusty white wings; greenish scales over underside of hind wing.

Caterpillar feeds on: Native mustard species, preferring the buds and flowers to leaves.

Similar species: Checkered white (*Pontia protodice*).

Habitat: Lowlands to mountains.

Mating flight: One in the north, two in the south, from April to September.

Distribution: Western North America; southern Canada in western mountains.

Becker's White

Pontia beckerii • Wingspan: 1.6–2 inches (4–5 cm)

A tenacious white butterfly that can survive in arid habitats where few other butterflies venture, and one that seems to be constantly on the move.

Identification: White uppers; more speckled with black in female form. The underside of the hind wing has radiating bands of mottled green, with a black mark on the center of the underside of its forewing.

Caterpillar feeds on: Plants of the mustard family and caper shrubs.

Similar species: Checkered white (*Pontia protodice*).

Habitat: Arid foothills, canyons, mountains.

Mating flight: Several, from May to September.

Distribution: British Columbia to Montana, from the central Rockies west to Southern California.

Large Marble

Euchloe ausonia • Also known as creamy marblewing • Wingspan: 1.5–2 inches (3.8–5.1 cm)

A wide-ranging butterfly found at low elevations in the Northwest. **Identification:** White-cream uppers with more extensive black markings on the forewing tip of females. The underside of the hind wing is mottled with a network of black and yellow scales.

Caterpillar: Hatches out onto unopened flower buds.

Caterpillar feeds on: Plants of the mustard family, including rock cress.

Similar species: California marble (*Euchloe hyantis*), northern marble (*Euchloe creusa*).

Habitat: Clearings, hillsides, meadows, and lowland areas.

Mating flight: One in the north, from May to July; two in lowland California, from February to August.

Distribution: From Alaska to Ontario, and south to northern New Mexico and southern California.

Olympia Marble

Euchloe olympia • Also known as olympia marblewing • Wingspan: 1.4–2 inches (3.5–5 cm)

A butterfly that is often seen in lakeshore dunes, with males flying fast and close to the ground. They often develop localized colonies.

Identification: One of its lesser names refers to the rosy tint to the undersides of the green-mottled hind wing; uppers are very pale.

Caterpillar: Eggs are laid singly.

Caterpillar feeds on: The flowers and fruits of a variety of rock cress.

Habitat: Meadows, clearings, shale grasslands, and lakeshore dunes.

Mating flight: One, from March to June. Earlier in the South.

Distribution: Central United States in a broad north–south band, and east into Virginia; sparingly in southern Canada.

Desert Orangetip

Anthocharis cethura • Wingspan: 1–1.6 inches (2.6–4 cm)

A vividly colored butterfly of arid regions, though if the overwintering pupa senses it is too dry, it can remain in the pupal stage for four years before emerging.

Identification: Orange tips are to the inside of black tips. White marks are dispersed in the black tips of the female; green marbled markings on undersides of hind wings.

Caterpillar feeds on: Plants of the mustard family, lace pod, and London rocket.

Similar species: Sara orangetip complex; Pacific, southwestern, and Stella orangetips.

Habitat: Rocky desert and chaparral country.

Mating flight: One, from February to May. Earlier in the South.

Distribution: California, Nevada, Arizona, and New Mexico.

Falcate Orangetip

Anthocharis midea • Wingspan: 1.4–1.8 inches (3.5–4.5 cm)

This is a small, delicate butterfly often seen flying slowly and close to the ground in early spring.

Identification: Has a characteristic hooked, or "falcate" forewing. Light mottled patterning on underside of hind wing. Only the male possesses the orange tip.

Caterpillar: Eggs are laid singly onto flower stalk.

Caterpillar feeds on: Plants of the mustard family.

Habitat: Along waterways, in damp woods and meadows.

Mating flight: One, from March to May. Earliest in the South.

Distribution: In a wide swathe from Texas to New England.

Clouded Sulphur

Colias philodice • Also known as common sulphur • Wingspan: 1.5–2.7 inches (3.8–6.9 cm)

One of the most widely distributed of butterflies, adults are likely to be spotted gathering at large mud puddles or on flowers.

Identification: Uppers are yellow with dark bands. There are white female forms, with pale yellow patches in a dark marginal band and orange spots in the centers of the upper hind wings.

Caterpillar: Larvae are cannibalistic, and green in color with a white stripe running along each side of the body. The white stripes may contain bars or lines of pink or orange.

Caterpillar feeds on: Many different legumes, alfalfa, and clover.

Similar species: Orange sulphur, western sulphur, and Christina's sulphur.

Habitat: Gardens, meadows, fields, and forests.

Mating flight: Two or three in the North, four or five in the South, from February to December.

Distribution: Most American states and Canadian provinces, with Quebec and Florida being exceptions.

Orange Sulphur

Colias eurytheme • Also known as alfalfa sulphur • Wingspan: 1.4–2.8 inches (3.5–7 cm)

The most widespread orange sulphur in America, it is less tolerant of cold, and so it is less prevalent than the clouded sulphur in Canada. They can be seen in "clouds" of butterflies above fields of alfalfa.

Identification: Orange-yellow uppers. These are more subdued in the female, which has yellow mottles in the black borders on wingtips—males do not. Lemon-yellow underside to hind wing.

Caterpillar feeds on: Many different legumes, alfalfa, and clover.

Similar species: Western sulphur, Christina's sulphur, common sulphur. Clouded and orange sulphurs often interbreed, creating a variety of forms.

Habitat: Gardens, meadows, fields, and roadsides.

Mating flight: Continuous, from March to December. Earliest in the South.

Distribution: Most of North America, except the western coast of Canada and the Far North.

Cloudless Sulphur

Phoebis sennae • Also known as cloudless giant sulphur • Wingspan: 2.2–3.2 inches (5.7–8.1 cm)

A butterfly of the southern states that migrates north in August and September.

Identification: Male is bright yellow, female is pale yellow or pale cream with dark margin; underside is lemon with reddish cloudy marks.

Caterpillar: Emerge onto young leaves or flower buds and rest on underside of leaf petioles.

Caterpillar feeds on: Senna and other cassia.

Similar species: Large orange sulphur (*Phoebis agarithe*).

Habitat: Gardens, scrubland, roadsides, meadows, and coasts.

Mating flight: Continuous in the South, temporary colonies farther north.

Distribution: Southern United States, migrating north toward the Great Lakes.

Southern Dogface

Zerene cesonia • Also known as dogface butterfly • Wingspan: 2.1–3 inches (5.4–7.6 cm)

Dogface sulphurs have a forewing pattern, vaguely suggestive of a poodle's head with a black eye when viewed from above.

Identification: Typical yellow "dog face" in the thick dark margin of both sexes, less pronounced in female. Male coloring is more intense.

Caterpillar feeds on: Legumes, clover, and indigo bushes.

Similar species: California dogface (*Zerene eurydice*).

Habitat: Open woodland, scrub, and short-grass prairie.

Mating flight: Three flights in the South, starting in May; vagrant in the North.

Distribution: Resident in southern and southwestern United States, migrating north to the Great Lakes, but not to the Northwest.

Dainty Sulphur

Nathalis iole • Also known as dwarf yellow • Wingspan: 0.8–1.3 inches (2–3.2 cm)

It's hard to spot this tiniest of the North American sulphurs in the wide-open habitats where it is found, flying just inches above the ground.

Identification: Has winter and summer forms. Female forewing black at the tip against a yellow background. Undersides of male are smoky or yellowish, with three black dots.

Caterpillar: Some larvae are dark green, while others are dark green with bright, pinkish-purple stripes.

Caterpillar feeds on: Dogweed and low-growing members of the daisy family.

Similar species: Little yellow (*Pyrisitia lisa*).

Habitat: Waysides, canyons, and deserts.

Mating flight: Continuous.

Distribution: From California to Florida across southern states. Northward as migrant to Canadian border.

Little Yellow

Pyrisitia lisa • Also known as little sulphur; formerly *Eurema lisa* • Wingspan: 1.3–1.7 inches (3.2–4.4 cm)

A common butterfly of the southeast that flies close to the ground, typically along weedy roadsides and field edges.

Identification: A little yellow butterfly, females sometimes are white or pale yellow, and both sexes have a black tip to the forewing.

Caterpillar: Eggs laid on mid-veins of host plants.

Caterpillar feeds on: Senna and other cassia plants.

Similar species: Dainty sulphur, barred yellow (*Eurema daira*).

Habitat: Dry, open areas with a weedy understory; vacant lots, roadsides, and meadows.

Mating flight: Continuous in south, from May to October in the North.

Distribution: From Texas east and northeast to the Great Lakes.

Gossamer Winged • *Lycaenidae*

Harvester

Feniseca tarquinius • Wingspan: 1–1.3 inches (2.5–3.2 cm)

A small, scarcely seen butterfly that sticks very close to its familiar habitat of stream borders and swamps, the harvester is never seen visiting flowers; the adult butterfly will sip honeydew but not nectar. It is also the only carnivorous butterfly in North America.

Identification: Orange with black/brown forewings; forewing margin bulges out slightly and the underside hindwing has many small circular marks toward the base.

Caterpillar: Ants will predate these larvae and so the caterpillar may hide under a silk mat covered with aphid carcasses.

Caterpillar feeds on: Woolly aphids and occasionally treehoppers and scale insects, which are all sap suckers. Adult females seek out alders along stream edges, along with witch hazel, hawthorn, beech, and ash.

Habitat: Damp woods.

Mating flight: Two in the North, from April to August; three in the South, from February to December.

Distribution: Eastern half of North America, as far west as Minnesota, north to the Great Lakes and the Maritimes, and south to central Texas and central Florida.

Gray Hairstreak

Strymon melinus • Wingspan: 0.9–1.4 inches (2.2–3.5 cm)

The most commonly found hairstreak in North America. A small gray butterfly spotted in a suburban environment is most likely to be a gray hairstreak.

Identification: Rich dark gray uppers with orange lunules between unequal tails. The underside is light or dark gray with a hairstreak line that fades from orange-white to blue. The abdomen is orange on males and gray on females. Unlike most others in the hairstreak tribe, they like to bask in the sun with their wings open.

Caterpillar feeds on: The flowers and fruits from a wide variety of flowering plants, particularly legumes. These include peas, beans, clover, and mallow.

Habitat: Exploits many man-made and natural habitats, preferring open sites.

Mating flight: Two in the North, from May to September; three or four in the South, from February to November.

Distribution: All across the contiguous United States and parts of southern Canada.

Coral Hairstreak

Satyrium titus • Formerly known as *Harkenclenus titus* • Wingspan: 1–1.5 inches (2.5–3.8 cm)

More likely to be seen with its wings folded, this hairstreak is more common in the East than in the West. The adult is particularly attracted to flowers of the butterfly weed.

Identification: Very dark brown, overpointed wings on male; the female is larger with rounded wingtips. The underside of the wing is caramel with a ring of orange lunules.

Caterpillar: Females lay eggs on twigs of host plant or in litter at base of the plant. Caterpillars remain in litter or camouflaged during the day, and emerge at night to feed on leaves and fruits. Eggs hibernate.

Caterpillar feeds on: Wild cherry and wild plum.

Similar species: Acadian hairstreak (*Satyrium acadica*) is similar but has a distinguishing tail that the coral lacks.

Habitat: Shrubby thickets, overgrown fields, and roadsides.

Mating flight: June–September.

Distribution: Across the contiguous United States and southern Canada, except the Pacific coast; along the Gulf Coast and Florida.

101

Banded Hairstreak

Satyrium calanus • Wingspan: 1–1.5 inches (2.5–3.8 cm)

The banded hairstreak is one of the most common hairstreaks found east of the Rocky Mountains. It is a territorial butterfly that will challenge many other butterflies invading its territory.

Identification: Rich dark brown on upper wings; male has a pronounced sex brand, a blue spot near the tail. Two rows of hairstreak lines cross the underside, which are more pronounced in the male.

Caterpillar: Eggs are laid on branches of the host during the summer, and hatch the following spring. Caterpillars eat catkins and leaves.

Caterpillar feeds on: Oak, walnut, and hickory.

Similar species: Hickory hairstreak (*Satyrium caryaevorum*).

Habitat: Waysides, open areas, and deciduous forest edges.

Mating flight: April to May in the South, June to July in the North.

Distribution: Eastern half of the United States, except the tip of Florida and parts of the Gulf Coast. Rocky Mountains, from Wyoming to northern New Mexico.

Striped Hairstreak

Satyrium liparops • Wingspan: 1-1.5 inches (2.6-3.8 cm)

Although they are widely distributed throughout the central and eastern United States and Canada, the striped hairstreak is not a common butterfly.

Identification: Rich dark brown on upper wing in both sexes, three broken hairstreak lines below, with orange and blue near two tails of the male.

Caterpillar: Eggs, laid singly on plant stems, hatch the following spring.

Caterpillar feeds on: Wild cherry, blueberry, oak, willow, hornbeam, and plants of the rose family.

Similar species: Edwards' hairstreak (*Satyrium edwardsii*) and king's hairstreak (*Satyrium kingi*).

Habitat: Urban fringe, deciduous forest edges, woodland clearings, and grassland streamsides.

Mating flight: From June to July in the North, from May to August in the South.

Distribution: From the Rocky Mountains eastward, including southern Canada, except the tip of Florida.

103

Great Purple Hairstreak

Atlides halesus • Also known as great blue hairstreak • Wingspan: 1.3–2 inches (3.2–5.1 cm)

A large and beautiful hairstreak displaying metallic colors, with one long and one short tail. This butterfly is quite solitary and spends a lot of its time in tree canopies.

Identification: Male is iridescent blue with a green base on forewings. Both male and female have red basal spots. The abdomen is orange.

Caterpillar feeds on: Mistletoe growing on a variety of trees, including oak, ash, poplar, juniper, and walnut.

Similar species: With wings folded up they look very different, but the upper wings resemble the white M hairstreak (*Parrhasius m-album*).

Habitat: Found in woodland where mistletoe infestations are greatest.

Mating flight: Two in the north, three in the south, from March to December.

Distribution: Concentrated in the southeastern and southwestern United States, rarely north of Missouri or Maryland.

Colorado Hairstreak

Hypaurotis crysalus • Wingspan: 1.2–1.5 inches (3.1–3.8 cm)

A butterfly with a drab underside and a vivid top; unlike a lot of hairstreaks, this butterfly will bask with its wings open. It is the state butterfly of Colorado.

Identification: Purple sheen over most of its forewings, and orange marginal marks. Underneath there is a W-shaped mark in one of the hairstreaks toward the tail (visible in the photo below). They have a slender, wispy tail.

Caterpillar feeds on: Gambel oaks. Adult butterflies will roost in the same tree and feed on honeydew produced by aphids or tree sap.

Habitat: Deciduous woodland containing gambel oaks.

Mating flight: June–September (varying with altitude).

Distribution: Utah, Colorado, Arizona, and New Mexico.

105

Juniper Hairstreak

Callophrys gryneus • Wingspan: 1–1.3 inches (2.5–3.2 cm)

Considered to be an evergreen hairstreak, the juniper hairstreak is never found too far from junipers or similar evergreens. They are widespread throughout the United States but show a great deal of color variation from east to west.

Identification: Gray-brown uppers with a suffusion of orange. Bright green or brown hind wing below crossed by white hairstreak marks and two pairs of unequal tails.

Caterpillar feeds on: Eastern red cedar and various juniper species.

Similar species: Hessel's hairstreak (*Callophrys hesseli*).

Habitat: Canyons and scarps, juniper woodland, and cedar breaks.

Mating flight: One in the North and the West, two in the South; from March to September.

Distribution: Throughout the contiguous United States, and sparingly in southern Canada, with a high concentration of populations to the west.

Hessel's Hairstreak

Callophrys hesseli • Also known as white cedar hairstreak • Wingspan: 1–1.1 inches (2.5–2.8 cm)

This hairstreak is seldom observed because of the swampy terrain it inhabits. Some populations are under threat from development.

Identification: Dark brown to reddish on uppers, vivid green speckled undersides with zigzagging, white irregular hairstreak line.

Caterpillar: Eggs are laid singly on terminal shoots of white cedar trees.

Caterpillar feeds on: Atlantic white cedar.

Similar species: Juniper hairstreak (*Callophrys gryneus*), although the Hessel's limited range and habitat make it easy to distinguish.

Habitat: Swamps and bogs containing white cedars.

Mating flight: One or two, dependent on latitude; May to July.

Distribution: Scattered populations along the Atlantic coastal plain from southern Maine to South Carolina and Georgia. Also found on the Gulf Coast of the Florida panhandle.

American Copper

Lycaena phlaeas • Wingspan: 0.9–1.4 inches (2.2–3.5 cm)

A brightly colored butterfly that may not actually be native to North America, despite its name. There are separate populations in the East and the West, and there are populations as far north as the Arctic Circle in Canada and Alaska.

Identification: Uppers are coppery, interspersed with dark spots; hind wings have coppery edges. The eastern variety is more vividly colored than its western form.

Caterpillar: The eggs are laid on the upper side of plant leaves and the young caterpillar feeds on the underside of the leaf, leaving the upper epidermis of the leaf intact. Pupation takes place on the ground in the leaf litter; the pupa is believed to be tended by ants.

Caterpillar feeds on: A variety of sorrel plants, such as sheep sorrel and dock leaves.

Similar species: Bronze copper (*Lycaena hyllus*).

Habitat: Flowery meadows, waste ground, and waysides.

Mating flight: One to three, dependent on latitude and altitude. Three flights in the South from April to September.

Distribution: Widely distributed across the northern United States and Canada, but with the greatest density of populations in the northeastern states. Absent from the Gulf Coast states.

Bronze Copper

Lycaena hyllus • Wingspan: 1.3–1.9 inches (3.2–4.8 cm)

The largest of the typical coppers, the bronze copper is most likely to be found in wet habitats in northern states. It resembles the American copper but it is larger and found on wetter sites.

Identification: A general coppery tone to uppers, but the male has a purple sheen with orange markings at rear of hindwing. The female is predominantly brown with splashes of orange on forewing. Underside of hind wing is gray-white.

Caterpillar feeds on: Water dock and curled dock.

Similar species: Gray copper (*Lycaena dione*).

Habitat: Damp meadows, ditches, streams, and freshwater marshes.

Mating flight: Two in the North and West, three to the south of its range in Oklahoma and Arkansas.

Distribution: North and northeastern states, and southern Canada. West to Wyoming, Colorado, and Alberta. Absent from Pacific, Gulf, and Atlantic coastal states south of North Carolina.

Ruddy Copper

Lycaena rubidus • Wingspan: 1.1–1.6 inches (2.9–4.1 cm)

This bright orange copper is resident in the northwestern United States, and populations often overlap with the distinctly different blue copper, both being found in damp habitats.

Identification: Upper is orange on forewing of males and lighter in females with darker spots. Undersides of both sexes are white, creating quite a contrast between its appearance when wings are folded and unfolded.

Caterpillar: Eggs are laid near the base of the host plant and overwinter.

Caterpillar feeds on: Dock leaves, sorrel, and knotweed.

Similar species: Ferris's copper (*Lycaena ferrisi*), which is limited to the White Mountains of Arizona.

Habitat: Sagebrush scrubland and streamsides in arid areas.

Mating flight: June–August (depending on altitude).

Distribution: From British Columbia and Alberta south to central California; northern New Mexico. East to the western Great Plains.

111

Blue Copper

Lycaena heteronea • Wingspan: 1.1–1.4 inches (2.9–3.5 cm)

The only blue-colored copper, this butterfly is often mistaken for a blue or azure, which are generally smaller. They are found at sea level in California but mostly at high elevations up to the treeline.

Identification: Male forewings are blue on uppers, female is usually brown. The undersides are white with black spots on the forewing.

Caterpillar: Young caterpillars will feed discreetly on the underside of leaves, while older ones consume the whole leaf.

Caterpillar feeds on: A variety of buckwheats.

Similar species: The males look similar to the males of the Melissa blue (*Plebejus melissa*) and Boisduval's blue (*Plebejus icarioides*), but they are more iridescent, more robust, and fly more rapidly.

Habitat: Sagelands, scrub, alpine meadows, and forest clearings.

Mating flight: June–August.

Distribution: Western contiguous United States, and southern British Columbia at the northern end of the range.

Purplish Copper

Lycaena helloides • Wingspan: 1–1.3 inches (2.5–3.3 cm)

A small, hardy copper with a purplish sheen that can still be found flying in late autumn in California.

Identification: Male has brown uppers with purple sheen on forewings, orange lunules around the edge of the hind wing. The female has dark orange spots around margins.

Caterpillar: Eggs are scattered in the litter below the host plant where they overwinter. Older caterpillars are grass-green in color with yellow stripes along back and sides and also obliquely on the sides.

Caterpillar feeds on: Knotweed, docks, sorrels, and cinquefoil.

Similar species: Dorcas copper (*Lycaena dorcas*), which is mostly found around the Great Lakes, across Canadian provinces, and up into Alaska.

Habitat: Meadows and waysides from sea level to the treeline.

Mating flight: Three or four in California, diminishing to one at altitude and at the northern end of its range. Up to three flights in eastern Colorado.

Distribution: From the Great Lakes to the Pacific Northwest and California. Absent from eastern and southern states.

113

Western Tailed Blue

Cupido amyntula • Wingspan: 0.9–1.1 inches (2.2–2.9 cm)

A small blue butterfly that is virtually identical to the eastern tailed blue (opposite), but whose ranges only marginally overlap—where they do, the western is found at higher altitudes. Older butterflies that have lost their tail are particularly difficult to identify.

Identification: Male with violet-blue uppers and single tail. Female has thicker dark border on forewing and orange lunules on hind wing. Pale underside of both sexes with rows of pale spots on forewing.

Caterpillar: Yellowish to dark green with a darker stripe down the back. They also have pink or red diagonal stripes and a pink lateral line. They overwinter as caterpillars.

Caterpillar feeds on: Milk vetches and other legumes.

Habitat: Roadsides, meadows, and clearings.

Mating flight: One or two, depending on latitude and altitude.

Distribution: Western states north to Alaska. Most of southern Canada.

114

Eastern Tailed Blue

Cupido comyntas • Also known as tailed blue • Wingspan: 0.8–1.1 inches (2.1–2.9 cm)

A common butterfly in the East that flies close to the ground. Because of its short proboscis, it must find flowers that have short tubes, so it is often seen feeding on the nectar of clover, wild strawberry, and asters. Males may gather at puddles around mud.

Identification: Male is violet-blue on uppers with distinct white edge outside of a black border. The female is brown with a single orange lunule. Both sexes have a single tail. Underside of hind wing is pale gray.

Caterpillar: Eggs are laid on the buds of flowers, and caterpillars will eat buds, flowers, and seeds. Hibernates as caterpillar and pupates in spring.

Caterpillar feeds on: A wide variety of legumes, clovers, vetches, and alfalfa.

Habitat: Managed grassland, pasture, parks, gardens, and roadsides.

Mating flight: Three in the North, from spring to fall; multiple in the South.

Distribution: Midwest to eastern states, with sizable pockets on the Pacific coast, and around southeastern Arizona and western New Mexico. Also extreme south of Canada and eastern Colorado.

115

Acmon Blue

Plebejus acmon • Also known as silver-studded blue • Wingspan: 0.7–1.1 inches (1.9–2.8 cm)

Above and opposite:

The more colorful male is shown above. The female, which is more brown in color, is shown opposite.

The acmon blue is found in a whole variety of habitats in the West. Males will often gather at mud banks. It is an elusive butterfly for experts to identify, as there are many variations of this and the lupine blue. It is versatile and good at colonizing new areas; it established a population on the slopes of Mount Saint Helens before the volcanic eruption of 1980.

Identification: Male has violet uppers, female is larger and with brown uppers. Both sexes have orange lunules around the margin of hind wing. The undersides are gray with orange lunules on hind wing.

Caterpillar: Young caterpillar overwinters; its mature form is dirty yellow, covered with fine white hair, a green back stripe, and a variety of lateral markings.

Caterpillar feeds on: Buckwheat, legumes, lupines, and bird's-foot trefoil.

Similar species: Lupine blue (*Plebejus lupini*), almost impossible to tell apart while they are free-flying.

Habitat: Many different areas including gardens, parks, meadows, fields, and roadsides. Almost everywhere except dense forests, which lack its host plant.

Mating flight: Multiple flights from March to October.

Distribution: Pacific coast states, from Baja California to Mexico, and western Washington.

Spring Azure Complex

Celastrina ladon • Wingspan: 0.9–1.4 inches (2.2–3.5 cm)

A butterfly that gained its name by its appearance in early spring, "spring azure" is actually a term that covers several forms that should be reclassified as separate butterflies in the future.

Identification: Male has sky-blue uppers, female is lighter blue with dark apex on forewings. Undersides are light blue-gray dispersed with small spots.

Caterpillar feeds on: A variety of woody shrubs, including dogwood and ceanothus. The caterpillars of different broods feed on different plants depending on which is flowering at the time. They are tended by ants.

Similar species: Summer azure, atlantic holly azure, hops azure, cherry gall azure, echo azure, and lucia azure.

Habitat: Woodland edges, old fields, swamps, and ditches.

Mating flight: Multiple in the South, but limited to May to August in Canada.

Distribution: From below the tundra line of Canada south to the Gulf of Mexico. Absent from the Texas coast and the tip of Florida.

Melissa Blue

Plebejus melissa • Also known as orange-bordered blue • Wingspan: 0.9–1.4 inches (2.2–3.5 cm)

This blue butterfly is a common sight in the West. There is a notable difference between the blue male and brown female.

Identification: Male has blue uppers, while two-thirds of the forewing of the female is brown, with blue at the base. The hind wing is mostly blue with pronounced orange lunules on the fore and hind wings. The underside is pale with an orange band.

Caterpillar: Eggs are laid on different areas of host plant, or in nearby leaf litter. They are tended by ants who feed on the extruded sugary secretions.

Caterpillar feeds on: Lupines, alfalfa, and other legumes of the pea family.

Similar species: Northern blue (*Plebejus idas*).

Habitat: Weedy wasteland, prairie, and lupine- or alfalfa-rich habitats.

Mating flight: Two or three, from May to August.

Distribution: Western half of the contiguous United States and Canada.

119

Metalmarks • *Riodinidae*
Mormon Metalmark

Apodemia mormo • Wingspan: 0.7–1.3 inches (1.9–3.2 cm)

The swift-flying Mormon metalmark likes to perch vertically, its head either up down, basking in the sun. The vivid colors of this butterfly integrate into the palette of its desert surroundings, making flying adults difficult to locate until they break cover.

Identification: White spots on uppers set against dark brown hind wing and chestnut base of forewing. Underside has repeat patterns of the uppers on a more subdued background color.

Caterpillar: Eggs are laid in groups of two to four on lower leaves of host plant, or singly on the stem. Caterpillars hide in shelters of leaves bound together with silk during the day, emerging at night to feed on leaves at first and stems when they are older. Mature caterpillar is dark gray-violet on back and sides, lighter below.

Caterpillar feeds on: Wild buckwheats and ratany.

Habitat: From sandy dunes to mountain slopes and rocky escarpments.

Mating flight: July to September in the North; March to October in the South.

Distribution: Entire west of the contiguous United States, from Montana to Arizona. Also northwestern Mexico and southwestern Canada.

Little Metalmark

Calephelis virginiensis • Wingspan: 0.5–1 inches (1.3–2.5 cm)

A tiny, brightly colored butterfly of the southeast Atlantic coastal plain that is easily overlooked, the little metalmark is one of the few butterflies that puts its antennae close together.

Identification: Russet uppers on male with black markings in close rows of dots and lines, with narrow metallic silver bands. The underside is tan.

Caterpillar: Caterpillars rest underneath leaves during the day, emerging at night or in subdued light to feed.

Caterpillar feeds on: Yellow thistle and vanilla plant.

Habitat: Grassy areas, clearings, and salt-marsh meadows.

Mating flight: Three in April to October; continuous in Florida.

Distribution: Atlantic coastal states from Maryland south to Florida and the Keys; west along the Gulf Coast to eastern Texas.

121

Brushfoots • *Nymphalidae*
Zebra Longwing

Heliconius charithonia • Also known as *Zebra Heliconian* • Wingspan: 2.8–3.9 inches (7–10 cm)

This beautiful and unusual butterfly eats pollen in addition to sipping nectar, which increases its longevity—up to three months as an adult. Males can detect a female chrysalis and will mate with the female as she emerges. A chemical deposited on her abdomen by the male will then repel other potential suitors. It will also return to roosts of twenty to thirty individuals in the evening. It is the state butterfly of Florida.

Identification: Long wings-to-body ratio, zebralike markings on both surfaces but of alternating yellow and brown colors, pale cream on undersides, and a red dot at base of hind wings.

Caterpillar feeds on: Passion vines (*Passiflora* species).

Habitat: Damp woodland and field edges, subtropical hammocks.

Mating flight: Continuous in the South.

Distribution: Southern states, principally Texas and Florida, rarely straying far north.

Great Spangled Fritillary

Speyeria cybele • Wingspan: 2.5–3.9 inches (6.3–10 cm)

The great spangled is the most commonly seen fritillary in the eastern United States. There is a wide geographical variation in forms, with many of the eastern butterflies hardly resembling examples from the western populations. The species is long-lived, and many individuals observed in late September have survived through the summer with worn and frayed wings.

Identification: Female is slightly larger than male, with large silver spangles on underside of hind wing. Uppers are orange with black markers, darker toward the base.

Caterpillar: Overwinters close to host plant and commences feeding in the spring.

Caterpillar feeds on: Violets.

Similar species: Aphrodite fritillary (*Speyeria aphrodite*), Atlantis fritillary (*Speyeria atlantis*), Nokomis fritillary (*Speyeria nokomis*).

Habitat: Meadows, woodland glades, and other moist, grassy areas.

Mating flight: June–September.

Distribution: Coast to coast in the United States and southern Canada, with limited numbers in the South.

Gulf Fritillary

Agraulis vanillae • Formerly known as *Dione vanillae* • Wingspan: 2.4–3.7 inches (6–9.5 cm)

This vividly colored butterfly takes its name from migrating flights of butterflies seen occasionally over the Gulf of Mexico.

Identification: Glittering silver underside spots, uppers are bright orange with black spots, and somewhat curved forewings.

Caterpillar: Grows to approximately 1.6 inches in length and is bright orange in color—covered in rows of black spines on its head and back. The conspicuous coloration is an indication that it is poisonous.

Caterpillar feeds on: Passion vines (*Passiflora*).

Habitat: Parks, gardens, pastures, and subtropical hammocks.

Mating flight: Continuous in the South.

Distribution: Southern states with migration northward. Resident in much of lowland California.

Variegated Fritillary

Euptoieta claudia • Wingspan: 1.8–3.2 inches (4.5–8 cm)

This low-flying fritillary is difficult to approach and is easily scared off. It is both widespread and a common sight in the South.

Identification: Female is larger. Soft orange colors interspersed with lines and dots of black on uppers; underside hind wing pattern is unique, with rich orange at base of forewing.

Caterpillar feeds on: Passion flowers, flax, violets, and other pasture plants.

Similar species: Mexican fritillary (*Euptoieta hegesia*).

Habitat: Meadows, roadsides, farmland, and brushy areas.

Mating flight: Continuous in the South; one in the North, from March to December.

Distribution: Southern states, spreading north to southern Canada in summer.

127

Aphrodite Fritillary

Speyeria aphrodite • Wingspan: 2–2.9 inches (5.1–7.3 cm)

A fritillary of the northern states and southern Canada, like many fritillaries it shows wide geographical variations in coloration between western and eastern forms.

Identification: Female is larger with rounder forewing tips. Orange uppers are speckled with black marks. The underside forewing pattern is a reversal of the uppers. The underside of the hind wing has a covering of silvery white spots.

Caterpillar: Overwinters close to host plant. Begins feeding in the spring.

Caterpillar feeds on: Plants from the violet family.

Similar species: Atlantis fritillary (*Speyeria atlantis*), great spangled fritillary (*Speyeria cybele*).

Habitat: Woods, wet meadows, and boggy areas.

Mating flight: June–September.

Distribution: From Nova Scotia west to the Rocky Mountains, then south to northern New Mexico. Absent in coastal states, except from Maryland to Maine.

Meadow Fritillary

Boloria bellona • Wingspan: 1.4–2 inches (3.5–5.1 cm)

Abutterfly that loves moist habitats. Common in the North and East, and, thanks to its versatility, it is gradually spreading its range farther south.

Identification: Forewing tip is slightly indented in male, otherwise dark orange-brown wings and a lack of highlighting on hind wing.

Caterpillar: Females lay greenish-yellow eggs, unusually on twigs or leaves other than the host food plant. Mature caterpillars are gray and black with small, light-colored spines.

Caterpillar feeds on: Violet species.

Similar species: Silver-bordered fritillary (*Boloria selene*), bog fritillary (*Boloria eunomia*), arctic fritillary (*Boloria chariclea*).

Habitat: Meadows, moist pastures, and wet aspen groves.

Mating flight: Three, from April to September.

Distribution: From the Yukon to Quebec in Canada, then south to northern Georgia. Also appears in Colorado, Wyoming, and Montana.

129

Hackberry Emperor

Asterocampa celtis • **Also known as hackberry butterfly** • **Wingspan: 1.4–2.5 inches (3.5–6.3 cm)**

A fast-flying butterfly that is widespread in the East and Midwest but more localized in the West. Adults perch upside down on tree trunks, well off the ground. There are many geographic color variations.

Identification: Forewings are rich brown with white marks. Rows of black spots are on inside margin of hind wing. The undersides are gray-brown with corresponding spots on hind wing.

Caterpillar: Eggs are laid in clusters on the host plant, and the young caterpillars feed communally. They also overwinter together in groups inside furled leaves.

Caterpillar feeds on: Various hackberries.

Habitat: Streamsides, woodland clearings, roadsides, parks, and gardens.

Mating flight: Three, from March to October.

Distribution: Most of the contiguous eastern United States and the Southwest.

Tawny Emperor

Asterocampa clyton • Wingspan: 1.7–2.8 inches (4.2–7 cm)

Like the hackberry emperor, this butterfly is firmly associated with its host plant, the hackberry. Both are seen flying erratically around these trees or getting minerals and moisture from the ground below.

Identification: Yellow to brown on uppers. Forewing has two solid chevronlike bars in a cell on the edge of forewing. Differs from hackberry in that it has no black spots on the upper forewing.

Caterpillar: Constructs a hibernaculum, or winter nest, by sewing hackberry leaves together and attaching it to the tree. As the trees drop their leaves for the winter, the hibernaculums stay on the tree.

Caterpillar feeds on: Hackberry trees.

Habitat: Waysides, parks, and gardens; anywhere supporting hackberries.

Mating flight: One in the North, two in the South, from March to October.

Distribution: Southeastern Arizona; New Mexico to Maine; Great Lakes and Florida.

131

American Snout

Libytheana carinenta • Also known as common snout or southern snout • Wingspan: 1.4–2 inches (3.5–5 cm)

The American snout is one of a kind, the only representative of the *Libytheana* subfamily in the United States. Incredible numbers of snouts migrating through Texas often make the news because of their sheer unpredictability, while adults can overwinter in the southern part of their range.

Identification: Snout butterflies have prominent elongated mouthparts (*labial palpi*). On the uppers there are large white spots and orange patches on brown squared-off forewings, plus an obvious orange patch on the hind wing. The underside of hind wing is gray.

Caterpillar feeds on: Hackberries.

Habitat: Streamsides, woodland clearings, roadsides, parks, and gardens.

Mating flight: Spring to fall in the North, continuous in the South.

Distribution: Southern United States, wandering north to the Great Lakes, New England, and the Great Plains.

Pearl Crescent

Phyciodes tharos • Wingspan: 0.8–1.3 inches (2.1–3.4 cm)

A familiar butterfly in the East; with so many similar crescent butterflies and a great deal of geographical variation—as well as seasonal variation—this can be a tricky butterfly to identify.

Identification: Uppers are very orange with dark margins around forewings. Hind wing has rows of orange spots and white lunules. In early spring and late fall, individuals can have lightish hind wings on the underside with heavier markings.

Caterpillar: Eggs are laid in small batches on the undersides of leaves. Caterpillars are gregarious when young, becoming solitary feeders as they grow older. They overwinter at the third instar stage.

Caterpillar feeds on: A variety of asters.

Similar species: Northern crescent (*Phyciodes cocyta*) has large, open orange areas on hind wing. The tawny crescent (*Phyciodes batesii*) is darker with a more checkered pattern.

Habitat: Meadows, fields, prairies, gardens, and roadsides.

Mating flight: Multiple in the North, from April to November; continuous in the South.

Distribution: From Alberta in Canada to Maine, and across the contiguous United States to Arizona. Absent from Pacific Northwest.

Northern Crescent

Phyciodes cocyta • Wingspan: 1.3–1.5 inches (3.2–3.8 cm)

A very similar butterfly to the pearl crescent, the northern crescent, on average, is slightly larger than the pearl crescent. As the name suggests, populations are centered in the northern states and across Canada.

Identification: Females are darker than males, whose antennal clubs are orange. Uppers are orange-brown with dark borders. Underside of hind wing is orange with a tan patch surrounding a pale, marginal crescent.

Caterpillar: Eggs are laid in batches of about forty on the underside of the host plant's leaves. Caterpillars are gregarious when young, becoming solitary feeders as they grow older. They overwinter at the third instar stage.

Caterpillar feeds on: Aster species.

Similar species: Pearl crescent (*Phyciodes tharos*), tawny crescent (*Phyciodes batesii*).

Habitat: Meadows, wooded streams, and marsh edges.

Mating flight: June–July.

Distribution: Spine of Rocky Mountains, Canada, and bordering U.S. states. South in the Appalachians to northern Carolina.

Mylitta Crescent

Phyciodes mylitta • Wingspan: 1.2–1.5 inches (3–3.8 cm)

The mylitta crescent is never far from thistles, neither does it venture much farther east than the Rocky Mountains. It can be found at sea level and up to 8,000 feet.

Identification: Small, with very light orange uppers and black marks. Female is darker, with forewing slightly indented. Underside is yellow-orange with indistinct rust-colored markings.

Caterpillar feeds on: A variety of thistles.

Similar species: Pale crescent (*Phyciodes pallida*), California crescent (*Phyciodes orseis*).

Habitat: Disturbed land where thistles can quickly colonize, meadows, fields, and vacant lots.

Mating flight: Two or three in the North, from March to October, and multiple in the South.

Distribution: British Columbia and Idaho south to California, Arizona, and New Mexico.

137

Silvery Checkerspot

Chlosyne nycteis • Wingspan: 1.4–2 inches (3.5–5.1 cm)

Larger than similarly colored crescents, the silvery checkerspot's flight is fast and direct in a series of rapid beats and glides.

Identification: Uppers are dark brown with orange and yellow markings. Underside hind wing has silvery basal band and white median band.

Caterpillar: Eggs are laid in batches of about a hundred on the underside of host plant leaves. Caterpillars feed in groups, decimating leaves as they go.

Caterpillar feeds on: Black-eyed Susan (*Rudbeckia*), sunflowers, and wingstem.

Similar species: Harris's checkerspot (*Chlosyne harrisii*), Gorgone checkerspot (*Chlosyne gorgone*).

Habitat: Ditches, streamsides, and damp meadows.

Mating flight: One in the North, from June to July; several in the South.

Distribution: From eastern slopes of Rocky Mountains eastward, excepting Florida. Straying into southern Canada.

138

Gorgone Checkerspot

Chlosyne gorgone • Also known as Great Plains checkerspot • Wingspan: 1.3–1.8 inches (3.2–4.5 cm)

A butterfly of the Great Plains, it is good at establishing isolated short-term colonies that ultimately die out.

Identification: Bright orange and brown uppers, the median band is very distinct on both pairs of wings and makes an obvious letter C.

The underside pattern of the hind wing is very busy. Veined wing cells can resemble a row of feathers on a headdress.

Caterpillar: Young caterpillars feed in groups before becoming solitary feeders.

Caterpillar feeds on: Sunflowers and crosswort.

Similar species: Silvery checkerspot (*Chlosyne nycteis*), Harris's checkerspot (*Chlosyne harrisii*).

Habitat: Prairies, flowery meadows, old fields, woodland edges, and waysides.

Mating flight: One in the North, two in the central region, and three at the southern end of its range, from April to October.

Distribution: Central provinces of Canada south through the Great Plains to central New Mexico, Texas, Louisiana, and Georgia.

139

Baltimore Checkerspot

Euphydryas phaeton • Also known as Baltimore • Wingspan: 1.7–2.7 inches (4.3–6.8 cm)

A distinctive butterfly like no other in the East, though there are geographical variations in hue. It was named after George Calvert, the first Lord Baltimore, whose family colors were orange and black. It is the state butterfly of Maryland.

Identification: Dark uppers with distinctive orange marginal marks, following inside with rows of pale yellow-white spots that are more enlarged in female. Female is larger than male and has more orange spots to the base of the underside hind wing.

Caterpillar: The heavily spined orange-and-black caterpillars spin a prehibernation web on a plant, stop feeding, and remain in the web. Several months later they leave this web and enter the litter (dead grass, leaves, etc.) on the ground, where they spend the winter.

Caterpillar feeds on: Turtlehead, false foxglove, and English plantain.

Habitat: Wet meadows, bogs, and deciduous woodland.

Mating flight: One, from May to August; earliest in the South.

Distribution: Primarily east of the Mississippi, with a concentration in the Northeast through Maine to southern Ontario, southern Quebec, New Brunswick, and Nova Scotia. Absent from Florida.

Variable Checkerspot

Euphydryas chalcedona • Also known as chalcedon checkerspot • Wingspan: 1.3–2.2 inches (3.2–5.7 cm)

A wide-ranging butterfly that can be seen all the way from the Alaskan coast down to Baja California. Given its name, it is hardly surprising that there are a great many variations by habitat type (such as desert).

Identification: Dark brown and cream uppers, like a checkerboard, with a tinge of red-orange. Underneath it has red-orange with cream and reddish marginal marks.

Caterpillar: Feeds communally on leaves and flowers. Third- and fourth-instar caterpillars overwinter under rocks or in leaf litter.

Caterpillar feeds on: Penstemon, snowberry, beardtongues, and paintbrush.

Habitat: Desert, chaparral, sagebrush flats, high prairie, open forest, and tundra.

Mating flight: May–June.

Distribution: Western Canada and United States from the Pacific Coast. East to Wyoming, Colorado, and New Mexico.

141

Red Admiral

Vanessa atalanta • Wingspan: 1.8–3 inches (4.5–7.6 cm)

A truly ubiquitous butterfly, the red admiral is found in most locations in North America up to the arctic tundra of Canada and Alaska. It can often be seen on migration flights in the East, while the warm Southwest allows adults to overwinter. It is one of the longest-lived butterflies, sometimes surviving for ten months.

Identification: Red-orange band crosses black forewing, which has white marks toward tip. There is a red-orange margin on the hind wing and the underside has a unique mottled pattern.

Caterpillar: Females lay eggs singly on the upper side of nettle leaves. Young caterpillars will eat and retreat to a shelter of folded leaves while older caterpillars will spin themselves a nest of leaves held together with silk.

Caterpillar feeds on: Plants of the nettle family, including stinging nettle and false nettle.

Habitat: All types, including urban, suburban, and rural.

Mating flight: One or two in the North, from spring to fall. Continuous in the South.

Distribution: The contiguous United States and southern Canada.

American Painted Lady

Vanessa virginiensis • Also known as American lady • Wingspan: 1.8–2.6 inches (4.5–6.7 cm)

The American painted lady, like its namesake (opposite), is a fast, erratically flying butterfly that migrates north in the summer, but not in the huge numbers that the painted lady amasses.

Identification: The key distinguishing feature is a pair of two large eyespots toward margins of the underside of hind wing. There is also a small white dot on the rear of the upper forewing that is not present on the painted lady.

Caterpillar: Females lay eggs singly on the upper side of host plant's leaves. Caterpillars create a nest of leaves tied with silk from which to feed.

Caterpillar feeds on: Everlastings, pussytoes, cudweed.

Habitat: Flowery waysides, streamsides, meadows, and parks.

Mating flight: Three or four in the North, from March to October; continuous in the South.

Distribution: Resident in the southern United States, temporarily colonizes the northern contiguous United States and southern Canada in the summer.

Painted Lady

Vanessa cardui • Wingspan: 2–2.9 inches (5.1–7.3 cm)

One of the most common and readily recognizable butterflies in North America, indeed around the world. They cannot endure constant temperatures below freezing point. They have northward flights when good winter rains produce masses of suitable hosts in northwestern Mexico. One of the reasons the painted lady is able to colonize so rapidly is because its caterpillars will feed on over a hundred different host plants.

Identification: Upper is orange-brown with black wing tips and variable-sized white spots within. Underside of hind wing has four unequal eyespots toward margin.

Caterpillar: Females lay eggs singly on the upper side of host plant's leaves. Caterpillars create a silk nest from which they emerge to eat plant leaves.

Caterpillar feeds on: Thistles, mallow, hollyhocks, fiddleneck, plus a huge variety of annuals.

Similar species: West Coast lady (*Vanessa annabella*).

Habitat: Almost any open flower-rich habitat, fields, pastures, gardens, parks, waysides, deserts, and suburbs.

Mating flight: One to three flights in the East, from April to October; three or four flights in the Southwest.

Distribution: Most of contiguous United States. Resident in the Southwest. North into Canada to edges of the Arctic Circle. Rare or absent in East and Southeast most years.

145

Mourning Cloak

Nymphalis antiopa • Wingspan: 2.2–4 inches (5.7–10.1 cm)

Their emergence signals that winter is over and spring is on its way, appearing as they do after the thaw sets in. It is one of the most distinctive butterflies and is hard to mistake for anything else. Adults prefer tree sap to flower nectar and will walk down the trunks of trees to feed with their head pointing down. The mourning cloak will hibernate as an adult, emerging again in spring to mate in early summer and create broods that will fly in the late summer to fall and then hibernate themselves. It is the state butterfly of Montana.

Identification: Strong cream-yellow border and a row of blue spots toward the margin of rich maroon-brown uppers. Undersides are dark with the same "petticoat" edging. Borders may fade to a paler cream-white color on older individuals.

Caterpillar: Eggs are laid in groups on the twigs of the host plant. Caterpillars are black and spiny, with fine white speckles and a row of much larger red spots running down the back. They live in a communal web and feed together on young leaves. Older caterpillars may wander onto non-host plants.

Caterpillar feeds on: Willows, cottonwoods, aspen, birches, hackberries, and American elm.

Habitat: Numerous types, from deciduous forest edge to urban environments (caterpillars will often pupate under concrete overhangs and awnings).

Mating flight: One, from June to July. Adults survive until the following spring. Occasionally there is a rare second brood in late summer.

Distribution: Most of North America, south of the tundra in Canada and Alaska, and south in the Mexican highlands. May overwinter in the warm Southeast and the Gulf Coast states.

Milbert's Tortoiseshell

Aglais milberti • Wingspan: 1.7–2.5 inches (4.2–6.3 cm)

Like their close relatives the commas, tortoiseshells have jagged wing edges, but the tortoise coloration is only apparent when their wings are folded. They also look very much like tree bark. Small numbers of adults may hibernate together.

Identification: Bright orange fire-effect bands across the uppers. Dark toward base inside dark margin punctuated with blue spots on hind wing. Forewing tip is squared off.

Caterpillar: Clumps of up to 900 eggs are laid on the underside of nettle leaves. Young instars feed communally, but older instars eat alone and make shelters from woven plant leaves.

Caterpillar feeds on: Plants from the nettle family.

Habitat: Streamsides, wet pasture, marshland, and waysides.

Mating flight: One or two, from May to August.

Distribution: Alaska to Newfoundland, southwest to California and New Mexico.

Compton's Tortoiseshell

Nymphalis vau-album • Wingspan: 2.5–3 inches (6.4–7.8 cm)

Another hibernating butterfly, the adults emerge in July, overwinter as an adult, and then mate in the following spring. They are larger than the similar comma.

Identification: Bold black marks set against orange background, with white marks near the tip and a characteristic white spot on the leading edge of hind wing.

Caterpillar: Clumps of eggs are laid on the underside of host plant leaves. Young instars feed communally.

Caterpillar feeds on: Willows, aspen, birches, and cottonwood.

Habitat: Clearings in upland forest, waysides, and streamsides.

Mating flight: One, from July to November, before hibernating.

Distribution: In a belt across northern United States and southern Canada, migrating both south and north in summer.

149

Viceroy

Limenitis archippus • Wingspan: 2.5–3.4 inches (6.3–8.6 cm)

Known as the "great impersonator," the viceroy butterfly mimics three butterflies: the monarch in the North; the queen in southern states, such as Florida, and Georgia, and in the Southwest; and the soldier butterfly in Mexico. Hence, there are many different variations to pin down.

Identification: Thin black line crosses veins of upper hind wing. Otherwise, rich caramel brown background color with black veins and white spots in dark marginal band on uppers.

Caterpillar: Caterpillars feed on catkins and leaves at night. They also make a ball of vegetation and dung, which they hang off leaves to distract potential predators.

Caterpillar feeds on: Willows, poplars, and cottonwood.

Habitat: Streamsides, meadows, waysides, and swamp edges.

Mating flight: Two or three, from May to September.

Distribution: Most of temperate North America, but far less common in California and the Pacific Northwest.

Red Spotted Purple

Limenitis arthemis astyanax • Wingspan: 2.5–3.4 inches (6.3–8.6 cm)

This is a schizophrenic butterfly—the white admiral has the same Latin name. Where their ranges meet and they interbreed, there are a great number of intermediate forms. Geographically, they are largely separated, with the white admiral taking Canada and Alaska, and the red-spotted purple from Ontario southward, with intermingling around the Great Lakes. The red-spotted purple is believed to mimic the pipevine swallowtail.

Identification: Intense dark blue on leading edge of forewing, fading to light iridescent blue on hind wing. Three conspicuous red spots on edge of wing tips. Red spots on edge of hind wings. Underside of forewing has purple tinge.

Caterpillar: Circular eggs are laid on the very tips of leaves. Caterpillar resembles bird droppings.

Caterpillar feeds on: Willows, poplars, oaks, cottonwood, basswood, and cherries.

Habitat: Woodlands and glades.

Mating flight: Two, from May to August.

Distribution: Eastern United States north to Great Lakes and Maine. Southwest from Arizona and New Mexico, south into Mexican highlands.

151

Question Mark

Polygonia interrogationis • Wingspan: 2.2–3 inches (5.7–7.6 cm)

This butterfly is most at home in a woodland setting, where it can make the most of its superb camouflage. However, this doesn't deter the question mark from migrating, especially in the East, and adults often stray from their breeding areas.

Identification: Key features are the long violet "tail" on the hind wing and the tiny white dot by a silver question mark on the underside of the hind wing (shown here to the left of where the legs meet the abdomen). There are also two forms: a darker summer form, which has a deeper black hind wing, and the winter form, which is a lighter color with more orange (opposite).

Caterpillar: Females lay stocks of 3–4 eggs under leaves of plants that may not be a host plant. Caterpillars must then find a host plant after they hatch. Adults of the second brood of the season, the winter form, overwinter. They breed the following spring to create the summer form, which in turn begets the winter form.

Caterpillar feeds on: American and red elm, hops, hackberry, and the nettle family.

Similar species: Eastern comma (*Polygonia comma*), satyr comma (*Polygonia satyrus*), gray comma (*Polygonia progne*).

Habitat: Woodlands, waysides, parks, and gardens.

Mating flight: Two, from May to September.

Distribution: Southern Canada from Saskatchewan east. Contiguous United States west to the eastern edge of the Rocky Mountains, south to southern New Mexico.

Eastern Comma

Polygonia comma • Wingspan: 1.8–2.5 inches (4.5–6.4 cm)

A butterfly of moist woodland; like the question mark, it has a winter and summer form. The summer form is darker on the hind wing upper than the winter form (photo shows winter form).

Identification: Outline of wings is highly indented with squared-off wing tips. Where there is a question mark on the underside hind wing of the question mark, there is a comma on the comma.

Caterpillar: Eggs are laid under host plant leaves or stems. Caterpillars are solitary and feed on leaves at night, emerging from shelters they weave for themselves with leaves.

Caterpillar feeds on: Nettles, hops, and American elm.

Similar species: Satyr comma (*Polygonia satyrus*), question mark (*Polygonia interrogationis*), gray comma (*Polygonia progne*).

Habitat: Deciduous woodland near rivers, marshes, and swamps.

Mating flight: Two, from March to October.

Distribution: Eastern North America, from Saskatchewan to Texas. Absent from peninsular Florida.

154

Hoary Comma

Polygonia gracilis • Also known as hoary anglewing • Wingspan: 1.5–2.2 inches (3.9–5.7 cm)

A butterfly of the West and Northwest with a more ragged wing outline than the previous two commas, but still neater than species such as the green comma or oreas comma. It is a butterfly that shows regional variation between its eastern and western forms.

Identification: Orange ground color with darker margins, light yellow marks inside margins, light outer part to hind wing. Undersides vary from gray to brown to mottled, but all with the small white comma on hind wing.

Caterpillar: Eggs are laid on leaves and leaf stems. Caterpillars eat leaves at night and rest below them during the day.

Caterpillar feeds on: Currants and gooseberries.

Habitat: Woodland clearings, forest, and mountain streamsides.

Mating flight: One, in July. Adults overwinter.

Distribution: From Alaska to California; east to Alberta and the Dakotas; south to New Mexico. Isolated populations in eastern Canada, Great Lakes, and Maine.

155

Buckeye

Junonia coenia • Also known as common buckeye • Wingspan: 1.7–2.8 inches (4.2–7 cm)

A butterfly with a variety of protective multicolored eyespots. Widespread through the United States but most common in the South. It has seasonal variations, with the spring form (left) lighter than the more intensely colored fall form (right). It will migrate northward in the summer into southern Canada.

Identification: Four eyespots on uppers of forewings (two large, two small), with four on hind wings (two very large and two smaller). Pale forewing bar enclosing the two larger eyespots. Underside of spring form is mottled brown while fall variation is more orange and leaflike.

Caterpillar: Eggs are laid singly on leaf buds or on upper surface of leaves. Caterpillars eat leaves and are solitary feeders.

Caterpillar feeds on: Plantains, figwort, snapdragons, and monkey plants.

Similar species: Mangrove buckeye (*Junonia genoveva*), tropical buckeye (*Junonia evarete*).

Habitat: Fields, meadows, and waysides.

Mating flight: Two or three in the North, from May to October; often continuous in Gulf Coast states.

Distribution: Pacific Coast, east along southern states to Southeast. Strays north irregularly to southern Canada and New England.

Goatweed Leafwing

Anaea andria • Also known as goatweed butterfly • Wingspan: 2.4–3.2 inches (6–8.2 cm)

A master of camouflage, the goatweed leafwing looks at home in the leaves of fall. Males are quite different from females with less patterning on uppers (left). Adults will migrate northward in the summer, breeding when they find larval food plants. There are summer and winter forms.

Identification: Male has bright reddish orange uppers, female is more subdued with lots of brown mottling and a darker area toward margins of its uppers; though undersides are similar. Both sexes have tails.

Caterpillar: Females lay eggs singly under host plant leaves. The young caterpillar lines itself up on a leaf midvein, then lives under the protection of a folded leaf, and finally nests in a rolled-up leaf.

Caterpillar feeds on: Goatweed, Texas croton, and prairie tea.

Similar species: Tropical leafwing (*Anaea aidea*), Florida leafwing (*Anaea troglodyta*).

Habitat: Deciduous woodland, waysides, field edges, and scrublands.

Mating flight: The winter form flies from August to April (overwinters); the summer form flies from July to August.

Distribution: From Arizona east to Florida. Primarily resident in the southern Great Plains and Mississippi River basin. Rarely strays north to eastern Wyoming, and no farther northeast than the Great Lakes.

Monarch

Danaus plexippus • Wingspan: 3.4–4.9 inches (8.6–12.4 cm)

One of the most famous butterfly species in the world. Migration flights of millions of monarchs—from eastern and central North America to the mountain forests of central Mexico—have become the subject of wildlife programs. Their migration is extraordinary. Individuals don't make the entire round trip and rely on instinct to find their way there. It is the state butterfly of eight states, from Texas to Vermont.

Identification: Large butterfly with rich orange-red ground color, black veins, and black border with two rows of white spots around wings.

Caterpillar: Eggs laid singly under the leaves of milkweeds. Caterpillars will eat both leaves and flowers. Most milkweeds contain cardiac glycosides, toxins which are stored in the bodies of both the caterpillar and adult, making them distasteful. Once tasted by a predator, they are thereafter avoided.

Caterpillar feeds on: Milkweeds such as common milkweed, swamp milkweed, and milkweed vine in the tropics.

Similar species: Mimicked by the viceroy butterfly.

Habitat: Flowery waysides, pastures, meadows, parks, and gardens.

Mating flight: One to three in the North; multiple in the South. Continuous in Florida and southern Texas.

Distribution: Southern Canada and the entire United States, except Alaska.

Queen

Danaus gilippus • Wingspan: 2.6–3.9 inches (6.7–9.8 cm)

Another important milkweed butterfly, but one that has to play second fiddle to the monarch. The queen is a butterfly of the South and it can even outnumber the monarch in Florida. It is resident in the Gulf Coast states and to the south of those states bordering Mexico, straying a long way north in summer but rarely along the Atlantic coastal plain, and never in a distinct migratory path like the monarch. The adults may roost communally.

Identification: Brown-orange ground color, black veins, and black border, with white spots around border. Not as heavily veined as the monarch. There are geographical variations between Florida and the Southwest, with the Florida male having a broader black border on the upper hind wing and no white spots. (Photo shows southwestern male.)

Caterpillar: Eggs are laid singly on leaves, stems, and flower buds; caterpillars consume them all.

Caterpillar feeds on: Milkweeds, such as common milkweed, swamp milkweed, and milkweed vine.

Similar species: The Florida viceroy (*Limenitis archippus floridensis*) mimics the queen; soldier (*Danaus eresimus*) and western viceroy (*Limenitis archippus obsoleta*).

Habitat: Many open habitats, including gardens, meadows, desert scrub, dunes, and waysides.

Mating flight: Continuous in the South; from July to August in the North.

Distribution: Coastal fringes of Atlantic and Gulf Coast states, southwestern United States. Sporadic sightings from Iowa west, south around the Great Lakes, and Mexico south to Central America.

Little Wood-Satyr

Megisto cymela • Wingspan: 1.1–1.9 inches (2.9–4.8 cm)

A butterfly with striking eyespots, the little wood-satyr frequents woodland edges. It appears in late spring, when it can be seen "bouncing" along close to the ground.

Identification: Two black eyespots with yellow rims on each forewing and hind wing are repeated on the underside of both. Hind wing spots may have smaller spots below. Two distinct lines cross the undersides of both wings.

Caterpillar: Eggs are laid singly on grass blades. The caterpillar body is light greenish brown with a dark dorsal line and alternating brown and yellowish lateral stripes. Fourth-stage instars overwinter.

Caterpillar feeds on: Grasses.

Similar species: There is a variation with larger eyespots known as "Viola's form." Carolina satyr (*Hermeuptychia sosybius*) and red satyr (*Megisto rubricata*) look similar with their wings folded.

Habitat: Damp woodland and field edges, subtropical hammocks.

Mating flight: One or two, from late spring to summer.

Distribution: Eastern part of the United States and into southeastern Canada.

164

Georgia Satyr

Neonympha areolata • Wingspan: 1.5–1.9 inches (3.7–4.9 cm)

With its wings open, this satyr of the Southeast can look quite drab, but with its wings closed it reveals an interesting eyespot variation.

Identification: Mid-brown uppers with no patterning at all. Underside of hind wing has five elongated eyespots varying in size inside orange oval. There are twin orange lines on the edge of forewing.

Caterpillar: Eggs are laid singly on larval host plant.

Caterpillar feeds on: Sedges.

Similar species: Helicta satyr (*Neonympha helicta*) is virtually identical but eyespots are less elongated.

Habitat: Sandy pine woods and marshland.

Mating flight: One brood from June to July in the North; two broods from April to fall in most of the range; multiple in Florida.

Distribution: Southeastern United States, from New Jersey to Florida on Atlantic seaboard, Gulf of Mexico states, and Arkansas.

165

Common Wood-Nymph

Cercyonis pegala • Also known as wood-nymph, large wood-nymph • Wingspan: 1.8–3 inches (4.5–7.6 cm)

A gorgeous large satyr of the woodland edge with many geographical variations to contend with. Adults visit mud, rotting fruit, dung, and, rarely, flowers.

Identification: Two large eyespots on forewing are repeated on underside. Variable-sized eyespots occur on both upper and underside of hind wing. The large patch of yellow visible on forewings below is typical of southeast variation; the western form retains the eyespots but lacks the yellow.

Caterpillar: Eggs laid singly on host plant leaves. Caterpillars hatch and immediately hibernate, only beginning to feed the following spring.

Caterpillar feeds on: Grasses.

Similar species: Mead's wood-nymph (*Cercyonis meadii*), great basin wood-nymph (*Cercyonis sthenele*).

Habitat: Parks and gardens, pastures, marshes, and subtropical hammocks.

Mating flight: One, from May to Ausgust.

Distribution: Most of the contiguous United States and southern Canada. Absent in southern Florida, northern Maine, and parts of the Southwest.

Northern Pearly-Eye

Enodia anthedon • Wingspan: 1.8–2.6 inches (4.5–6.7 cm)

This fast-flying satyr keeps to the shadows and is the almost-identical twin to the southern pearly-eye, which has a different larval host plant and is confined to the South.

Identification: Forewing eyespots are arranged nearly in a straight line. The spots on the underside are not so pronounced. There are fewer dark markings than on the southern pearly-eye.

Caterpillar: Eggs are laid singly on the host plant.

Caterpillar feeds on: Various grasses and bottlebrush.

Similar species: Southern pearly-eye (*Enodia portlandia*), creole pearly-eye (*Enodia creola*).

Habitat: Waysides, clearings, woodlands, and creeks.

Mating flight: One brood in the North from June to August; two broods in the South from April to September.

Distribution: In Canada, from Saskatchewan eastward. In the United States, from Nebraska eastward. Very rarely strays into the Deep South.

Common Alpine

Erebia epipsodea • Wingspan: 1.7–2 inches (4.2–5.1 cm)

Alpines are dusky satyrs and fly close to the ground. The common alpine is the most frequently spotted in the West and is typically found in mountain meadows.

Identification: Dark wings with twin spots on forewing and other spots both on forewing and hind wing, all set in a band of pale red-orange. Undersides have a dark chocolate coloration and spots on the hind wing distinguish it from other alpines.

Caterpillar: Eggs are laid on living or dead grasses, forcing young instars to find a more nutritious host plant.

Caterpillar feeds on: Grasses.

Similar species: Vidler's alpine (*Erebia vidleri*).

Habitat: Alpine meadows, moist grassland, and high prairie.

Mating flight: June–August.

Distribution: From Alaska through the spine of the Rocky Mountains to New Mexico, and east across Canadian prairie provinces.

Red-disked Alpine

Erebia discoidalis • Also known as red disk • Wingspan: 1.5–1.9 inches (3.8–4.9 cm)

This butterfly comes with its own furry body warmer! The red-disked alpine inhabits some of the northernmost regions, where temperature is critical to the timing of pupation.

Identification: Named after a red flush on the forewing. Otherwise, its overall color is ruddy brown, with no patterning on uppers or underside.

Caterpillar: Eggs are laid singly on host plant. Fourth-stage instars hibernate, often missing years in a state of diapause.

Caterpillar feeds on: Bluegrass and sedges.

Similar species: Banded alpine (*Erebia fasciata*), magdalena alpine (*Erebia magdalena*).

Habitat: Wet meadows, bogs, and marshy areas.

Mating flight: May–July.

Distribution: From Alaska, south and east to Alberta as far as Quebec. Includes northern parts of Montana, Wisconsin, and Michigan.

169

Skippers • *Hesperiidae*
Yucca Giant-skipper

Megathymus yuccae • Also known as yucca skipper • Wingspan: 1.9–3.1 inches (4.8–7.9 cm)

This skipper can be found across the southern states, but sightings of adults are rare. It is the most widespread of the North American giant-skippers, which all have caterpillars that bore into their host plant's roots or leaves and remain there for the pupation process.

Identification: White wedge toward tip of forewings is a key feature. Male is smaller than female with fewer orange markings on upper hind wings.

Caterpillar: Eggs are laid singly on young host plants. Early instars feed near the tips of leaves. Older caterpillars bore into the root, making a silk chimney or tent that projects from the growing point of the plant. Mature caterpillars overwinter in their chimneys and pupate within, either in late winter or early spring.

Caterpillar feeds on: Joshua tree, Spanish bayonet, Spanish dagger, and a variety of other yuccas.

Similar species: Strecker's giant-skipper (*Megathymus streckeri*), ursine giant skipper (*Megathymus ursus*).

Habitat: Limited to areas that have significant quantities of yucca plants: deserts, canyons, and scrubland.

Mating flight: February–June.

Distribution: East to west across southern states, through north to Utah and Nebraska in mountainous regions and the Great Plains.

Strecker's Giant-skipper

Megathymus streckeri • Also known as plains giant-skipper • Wingspan: 2.2–3 inches (5.7–7.8 cm)

A giant-skipper of the prairie grasslands that is slightly larger than the yucca giant-skipper. The ursine giant-skipper is the biggest of all. Adults do not feed but instead rely on fat stores, although males may also sip moisture from mud puddles or wet sand.

Identification: The female is larger than the male with whitish-cream markings on forewing and pale straw markings as a row and on margin of hind wing. This row is absent in the male. Distinctive long hairs on upper hind wing and lower forewing.

Caterpillar: Eggs laid singly on leaves of host plant. Early instars burrow straight into the root without making a tent (like the yucca giant-skipper). After overwintering in the hole they have eaten away, the caterpillar emerges and constructs a tent of silk, soil, and plant fragments in which to pupate. The chrysalides are able to move up and down within the tent.

Caterpillar feeds on: Plants from yucca family, including small soapweed.

Habitat: Sandy prairie, scrubland.

Mating flight: May–July.

Distribution: Two bulges of population, one centering on New Mexico and its bordering states, the other centering on South Dakota and its bordering states, including the northeastern corner of Colorado.

171

Common Checkered-Skipper

Pyrgus communis • Wingspan: 1–1.5 inches (2.5–3.8 cm)

Chances are if you see a skipperlike butterfly out and about, it's most likely to be this one. The common checkered-skipper is the most widespread skipper in North America and is found in a great variety of habitats, from sea level to the mountains. Adults usually rest with their wings open.

Identification: A gray background color with white checkering, the male (above) is more intricately checkered over the uppers than the female (opposite). Underside is very pale with similar checkered pattern and distinct off-white band. There are color form variations with a light brown upper and also a light brown underside. It can only be separated from the white checkered-skipper by dissection.

Caterpillar: Eggs are laid singly on leaf buds and tops of leaves. Caterpillars make nests from folded woven leaves in which they live and feed. Mature caterpillars will overwinter.

Caterpillar feeds on: Mallows, hollyhocks, and abutilon.

Similar species: White checkered-skipper (*Pyrgus albescens*), tropical checkered-skipper (*Pyrgus oileus*), and desert checkered-skipper (*Pyrgus philetas*).

Habitat: Meadows, fields, waysides, woodland clearings, and a variety of sunny open habitats.

Mating flight: All year in Texas; March to September in the North.

Distribution: Most of the contiguous United States and southern Canada, with the exception of the colder northern New England states. It is now generally absent from southern California, southern New Mexico, the Gulf Coast, Florida, and the South Atlantic Coastal Plain, where it has been replaced by the white checkered-skipper.

Silver-spotted Skipper

Epargyreus clarus • Wingspan: 1.8–2.6 inches (4.5–6.7 cm)

An easily identified and common skipper, the adults often perch with their wings closed to reveal the silver patch that gives them their name.

Identification: A large silver spot is very obvious on underside of hind wing. Wings are rich brown in color with golden forewing marks.

Caterpillar: Eggs are laid singly near the host trees, requiring caterpillars to find the correct edible host plant. Young caterpillars are green and live in a folded leaf; older instars create a nest of woven leaves.

Caterpillar feeds on: Locust plants, false indigo, wisteria, and some herbaceous legumes.

Similar species: Viewed from above with wings unfolded, they resemble the golden-banded skipper (*Autochton cellus*).

Habitat: Woodland clearings, canyons, and prairies.

Mating flight: One to two, from spring to fall.

Distribution: Southernmost Canada and most of the contiguous United States, except the Great Basin and western Texas.

Southern Cloudywing

Thorybes bathyllus • Wingspan: 1.2–1.4 inches (3–3.5 cm)

One of four similar dark skippers that includes the northern cloudywing, the california cloudywing, and the confused cloudywing, which are difficult to tell apart. There is an added level of difficulty in the South, where the southern cloudywing produces a spring and summer form.

Identification: Dark brown background color on uppers with a single white mark on outer edge of forewing. Inside this is a line of white spots from the edge of the forewing (with a slight variation in the summer form). Both white marks are visible on the underside.

Caterpillar: Pale green eggs are laid singly on the underside of host plant leaves. Caterpillar is brown with a greenish hue, a dark middorsal stripe, and a pale lateral line. The head and collar are both black. They roll a silk-tied leaf shelter for themselves.

Caterpillar feeds on: Clover, tick trefoils, wild beans, and hog peanut.

Habitat: A variety of open habitats: meadows, clearings, and savanna.

Mating flight: One in the North, from June to July. Two in the South, from June to October.

Distribution: Most of the eastern United States, west to Nebraska, Texas, and Wisconsin.

Northern Cloudywing

Thorybes pylades • Wingspan: 1.3–1.9 inches (3.2–4.7 cm)

Slighty larger than the southern cloudywing, this skipper is both more common and more widespread in North America, reaching to both the Atlantic and Pacific seaboards.

Identification: Dark brown-black on uppers with small white marks dotted on forewing. Whereas they form a line on the southern cloudywing, on the northern they are haphazard; similar coloration on undersides. West Texan variation has white frosting to underside of hind wing.

Caterpillar: Pale green eggs are laid singly on the underside of host plant leaves. Caterpillars feed on leaves only and occupy rolled-leaf shelters, which they bind with silk.

Caterpillar feeds on: Beggar's tick, bush clover, lotus, wild beans, and other members of the pea family.

Similar species: California cloudywing (*Thorybes diversus*).

Habitat: Woodland clearings, forest edges, and scrubland.

Mating flight: One in the north, from June to July; earlier in the South. Two in Texas.

Distribution: Most of the contiguous United States and southern Canada, though scarce in the Great Basin and southern Great Plains.

177

Long-tailed Skipper

Urbanus proteus • Also known as bean leafroller • Wingspan: 1.8–2.4 inches (4.5–6.1 cm)

The most common tailed skipper, limited to breeding in the more temperate areas of the South, but straying north in summer. The caterpillar is regarded as an agricultural pest because it eats bean crops.

Identification: A showy butterfly, with wings of light brown tinted with iridescent blue (veering toward turquoise), and two long tails extending from the hind wings. The robust abdomen is light blue to blend in with blue coloration on uppers; brown undersides.

Caterpillar: Females lay eggs under leaves of host plants in clumps of up to twenty. Caterpillars feed on leaves and roll leaves up to form shelters (hence their alternative name).

Caterpillar feeds on: Many legumes, including vine legumes and various beans, hog peanuts, beggar's tick, and wisteria.

Habitat: Fields, woodland edges, gardens, and a variety of open habitats.

Mating flight: Continuous in the South. Two or three broods throughout the year in Florida, southern Texas, and southern Arizona.

Distribution: Gulf and Atlantic coast north to Connecticut. Inland to southern Illinois, and eastern Kansas. They rarely stray into southern Arizona and Southern California from Mexico.

Common Sootywing

Pholisora catullus • Also known as roadside rambler • Wingspan: 1–1.3 inches (2.5–3.3 cm)

This is the most familiar small black skipper. They fly slowly and close to the ground, and are often seen on waysides.

Identification: Small black butterfly with rounded wings and black underside. Tiny white spots sprinkled across outer forewing of uppers. Some have a few peppered white marks on hind wing, and some forms are more a deeper brown than black.

Caterpillar: Eggs are laid singly on upper side of host plant leaves. Caterpillars live and feed from within folded leaves. Mature caterpillars of second brood overwinter in leaf shelters and pupate within them in spring.

Caterpillar feeds on: Pigweeds and lamb's quarters weeds.

Similar species: Mexican sootywing (*Pholisora mejicanus*), Mojave sootywing (*Pholisora libya*).

Habitat: Disturbed ground, weedy areas, roadsides, and field edges.

Mating flight: Two, from May to September.

Distribution: Most of the contiguous United States, plus British Columbia and Quebec. Absent in northern Maine.

Hayhurst's Scallopwing

Staphylus hayhurstii • Wingspan: 1–1.3 inches (2.5–3.2 cm)

Scallopwings are small, dark skippers with scalloped outer hind wings. Hayhurst's scallopwing is widespread in the East but is not an abundant butterfly.

Identification: Dark brown to black background color with barklike mottling on uppers and a handful of white spots dotted across outer forewing.

Caterpillar: Eggs are laid singly on underside of host plant leaves. Caterpillars feed at night and rest in leaf rolls during the day. Third-stage caterpillars overwinter in tightly silked dead leaf rolls.

Caterpillar feeds on: Lambsquarters and chaff flower.

Similar species: Mazans scallopwing (*Staphylus mazans*).

Habitat: Waysides, woodland clearings, vacant lots, and gardens.

Mating flight: Two broods from May to August in most of its range; February to December in Florida.

Distribution: From Nebraska and eastern Colorado, south to central Texas, southeast to Florida, and east to Maryland.

181

Juvenal's Duskywing

Erynnis juvenalis • Wingspan: 1.3–1.9 inches (3.2–4.9 cm)

A difficult butterfly to identify with certainty because of geographical variations, and also due to the difference between males and females, though its singular habitat of oak woodland is one guide.

Identification: Forewing is gray-brown and a mottled pattern on uppers. Hind wing pattern and coloration is distinctly different from forewing. Hind wing underside has two white spots near margin.

Caterpillar: Eggs are laid singly on young leaves of the host plants. Caterpillars eat leaves and rest in nests of rolled or tied leaves.

Caterpillar feeds on: Oak trees.

Similar species: Horace's duskywing (*Erynnis horatius*).

Habitat: Oak woodland.

Mating flight: April–June.

Distribution: Eastern part of the United States and Canada down to Texas, with pockets in Arizona and New Mexico.

Sleepy Duskywing

Erynnis brizo • Wingspan: 1.3–1.8 inches (3.2–4.5 cm)

A butterfly of early spring. The sleepy is quite large for a duskywing, larger than a similar species, the dreamy duskywing. They are the only two duskywings without white forewing spots.

Identification: Mottled gray forewings with distinct wavy band on uppers. Hind wing is light brown with rows of faint spots toward margin.

Caterpillar: Eggs are laid on young leaves or leaf buds of host plant. Caterpillars feed on leaves and rest in leaf shelters.

Caterpillar feeds on: Scrub oak.

Similar species: Dreamy duskywing (*Erynnis icelus*), Rocky Mountain duskywing (*Erynnis telemachus*), persius duskywing (*Erynnis persius*).

Habitat: Oak woodland and chaparral.

Mating flight: One in the South, from January to May; March to June elsewhere.

Distribution: Most of the contiguous United States, with the exception of the Pacific Northwest. From southern Manitoba to southern Ontario in Canada.

183

Complete List of
North American Butterflies

Swallowtails (Papilionidae)

Parnassians (Parnassiinae)
Eversmann's parnassian (*Parnassius eversmanni*)
Clodius parnassian (*Parnassius clodius*)
Phoebus parnassian (*Parnassius phoebus*)
Sierra Nevada parnassian (*Parnassius behrii*)
Rocky Mountain parnassian (*Parnassius smintheus*)

True Swallowtails (Papilioninae)
White-dotted cattleheart (*Parides alopius*)
True cattleheart (*Parides eurimedes*)
Pipevine swallowtail (*Battus philenor*)
Polydamas swallowtail (*Battus polydamas*)
Zebra swallowtail (*Eurytides marcellus*)
Old World swallowtail (*Papilio machaon*)
Short-tailed swallowtail (*Papilio brevicauda*)
Ozark swallowtail (*Papilio joanae*)
Black swallowtail (*Papilio polyxenes*)
Anise swallowtail (*Papilio zelicaon*)
Indra swallowtail (*Papilio indra*)
Asian swallowtail (*Papilio xuthus*)
Canadian tiger swallowtail (*Papilio canadensis*)
Appalachian tiger swallowtail (*Papilio appalachiensis*)
Eastern tiger swallowtail (*Papilio glaucus*)
Mexican tiger swallowtail (*Papilio alexiares*)
Western tiger swallowtail (*Papilio rutulus*)
Pale tiger swallowtail (*Papilio eurymedon*)
Two-tailed tiger swallowtail (*Papilio multicaudata*)
Three-tailed tiger swallowtail (*Papilio pilumnus*)
Spicebush swallowtail (*Papilio troilus*)
Palamedes swallowtail (*Papilio palamedes*)
Magnificent swallowtail (*Papilio garamas*)
Victorine swallowtail (*Papilio victorinus*)
Giant swallowtail (*Papilio cresphontes*)
Thoas swallowtail (*Papilio thoas*)
Broad-banded swallowtail (*Papilio astyalus*)
Ornythion swallowtail (*Papilio ornythion*)
Androgeus swallowtail (*Papilio androgeus*)
Schaus's swallowtail (*Papilio aristodemus*)
Bahamian swallowtail (*Papilio andraemon*)
Ruby-spotted swallowtail (*Papilio anchisiades*)
Pink-spotted swallowtail (*Papilio rogeri*)

Whites and Sulphurs (Pieridae)

Mimic-whites (Dismorphinae)
Costa-spotted mimic-white (*Enantia albania*)

Sulphurs and yellows (Coliadinae)
Lyside sulphur (*Kricogonia lyside*)
Dainty sulphur (*Nathalis iole*)
Barred yellow (*Eurema daira*)
Boisduval's yellow (*Eurema boisduvaliana*)
Mexican yellow (*Eurema mexicana*)
Salome yellow (*Eurema salome*)
Sleepy orange (*Abaeis nicippe*)
Tailed orange (*Pyrisitia proterpia*)
Little yellow (*Pyrisitia lisa*)
Mimosa yellow (*Pyrisitia nise*)
Dina yellow (*Pyrisitia dina*)
Whitish yellow (*Pyrisitia messalina*)
Clouded sulphur (*Colias philodice*)

Orange sulphur (*Colias eurytheme*)
Western sulphur (*Colias occidentalis*)
Christina's sulphur (*Colias christina*)
Queen Alexandra's sulphur (*Colias alexandra*)
Harford's sulphur (*Colias harfordii*)
Mead's sulphur (*Colias meadii*)
Johansen's sulphur (*Colias johanseni*)
Hecla sulphur (*Colias hecla*)
Canadian sulphur (*Colias canadensis*)
Booth's sulphur (*Colias tyche*)
Labrador sulphur (*Colias nastes*)
Scudder's sulphur (*Colias scudderii*)
Giant sulphur (*Colias gigantea*)
Pelidne sulphur (*Colias pelidne*)
Pink-edged sulphur (*Colias interior*)
Palaeno sulphur (*Colias palaeno*)
Sierra sulphur (*Colias behrii*)
Southern dogface (*Zerene cesonia*)
California dogface (*Zerene eurydice*)
White angled-sulphur (*Anteos clorinde*)
Yellow angled-sulphur (*Anteos maerula*)
Cloudless sulphur (*Phoebis sennae*)
Pale apricot sulphur (*Phoebis argante*)
Large orange sulphur (*Phoebis agarithe*)
Orange-barred sulphur (*Phoebis philea*)
Tailed sulphur (*Phoebis neocypris*)
Statira sulphur (*Aphrissa statira*)
Orbis sulphur (*Aphrissa orbis*)

Whites (Pierinae)
Desert orangetip (*Anthocharis cethura*)
Sara orangetip (*Anthocharis sara*)
Falcate orangetip (*Anthocharis midea*)
Gray Marble (*Anthocharis lanceolata*)
Large Marble (*Euchloe ausonides*)
Arctic Marble (*Euchloe naina*)
Olympia Marble (*Euchloe olympia*)
Northern Marble (*Euchloe creusa*)
California Marble (*Euchloe hyantis*)
Desert Marble (*Euchloe lotta*)
Sonoran Marble (*Euchloe guaymasensis*)
Florida white (*Glutophrissa drusilla*)
Creamy white (*Melete lycimnia*)
Pine white (*Neophasia menapia*)
Mexican pine white (*Neophasia terlooii*)
Mexican dartwhite (*Catasticta nimbice*)
Viardi white (*Pieriballia viardi*)
Black-banded white (*Itaballia demophile*)
Mountain white (*Leptophobia aripa*)
Arctic white (*Pieris angelika*)
Margined white (*Pieris marginalis*)
Mustard white (*Pieris oleracea*)
West Virginia white (*Pieris virginiensis*)
Cabbage white (*Pieris rapae*)
Becker's white (*Pontia beckerii*)
Checkered white (*Pontia protodice*)
Western white (*Pontia occidentalis*)
Spring white (*Pontia sisymbrii*)
Great Southern white (*Ascia monuste*)
Giant white (*Ganyra josephina*)
Howarth's white (*Ganyra howarthi*)

Gossamer Winged (Lycaenidae)

Harvesters (Miletinae)
Harvester (*Feniseca tarquinius*)

Coppers (Lycaeninae)
American copper (*Lycaena phlaeas*)
Lustrous copper (*Lycaena cupreus*)
Tailed copper (*Lycaena arota*)
Hermes copper (*Lycaena hermes*)
Edith's copper (*Lycaena editha*)
Great copper (*Lycaena xanthoides*)
Gray copper (*Lycaena dione*)
Gorgon copper (*Lycaena gorgon*)
Ruddy copper (*Lycaena rubidus*)
Blue copper (*Lycaena heteronea*)
Bronze copper (*Lycaena hyllus*)
Bog copper (*Lycaena epixanthe*)
Dorcas copper (*Lycaena dorcas*)
Dos Passos' copper (*Lycaena dospassosi*)
Purplish copper (*Lycaena helloides*)
Lilac-bordered copper (*Lycaena nivalis*)
Mariposa copper (*Lycaena mariposa*)

Hairstreaks (Theclinae)
Colorado hairstreak (*Hypaurotis crysalus*)
Golden hairstreak (*Habrodais grunus*)
Mexican cycadian (*Eumaeus toxea*)
Atala (*Eumaeus atala*)
Great blue hairstreak (*Atlides halesus*)
Gold-bordered hairstreak (*Rekoa palegon*)
Marius hairstreak (*Rekoa marius*)
Creamy hairstreak (*Arawacus jada*)
Western sooty hairstreak (*Satyrium fuliginosa*)
Sagebrush sooty hairstreak (*Satyrium semiluna*)
Behr's hairstreak (*Satyrium behrii*)
Acadian hairstreak (*Satyrium acadica*)
California hairstreak (*Satyrium californica*)
Sylvan hairstreak (*Satyrium sylvinus*)
Coral hairstreak (*Satyrium titus*)
Edwards's hairstreak (*Satyrium edwardsii*)
Banded hairstreak (*Satyrium calanus*)
Hickory hairstreak (*Satyrium caryaevorus*)
King's hairstreak (*Satyrium kingi*)
Striped hairstreak (*Satyrium liparops*)
Gold-hunter's hairstreak (*Satyrium auretorum*)
Mountain mahogany hairstreak (*Satyrium tetra*)
Hedgerow hairstreak (*Satyrium saepium*)
Oak hairstreak (*Satyrium favonius*)
Ilavia hairstreak (*Satyrium ilavia*)
Poling's hairstreak (*Satyrium polingi*)
Soapberry hairstreak (*Phaeostrymon alcestis*)
Silver-banded hairstreak (*Chlorostrymon simaethis*)
Amethyst hairstreak (*Chlorostrymon maesites*)
Telea hairstreak (*Chlorostrymon telea*)
Goodson's greenstreak (*Cyanophrys goodsoni*)
Tropical greenstreak (*Cyanophrys herodotus*)
Clench's greenstreak (*Cyanophrys miserabilis*)
Western green hairstreak (*Callophrys affinis*)
Sheridan's hairstreak (*Callophrys sheridanii*)
Lotus hairstreak (*Callophrys perplexa*)
Juniper hairstreak (*Callophrys gryneus*)
Muir's hairstreak (*Callophrys muiri*)
Thorne's hairstreak (*Callophrys thornei*)

Hessel's hairstreak (*Callophrys hesseli*)
Xami hairstreak (*Callophrys xami*)
Sandia hairstreak (*Callophrys mcfarlandi*)
Thicket hairstreak (*Callophrys spinetorum*)
Johnson's hairstreak (*Callophrys johnsoni*)
Brown elfin (*Callophrys augustinus*)
Desert elfin (*Callophrys fotis*)
Moss's elfin (*Callophrys mossii*)
Hoary elfin (*Callophrys polios*)
Frosted elfin (*Callophrys irus*)
Henry's elfin (*Callophrys henrici*)
Bog elfin (*Callophrys lanoraieensis*)
Eastern pine elfin (*Callophrys niphon*)
Western pine elfin (*Callophrys eryphon*)
Strophius hairstreak (*Allosmaitia strophius*)
Ruddy hairstreak (*Electrostrymon hugon*)
Muted hairstreak (*Electrostrymon joya*)
Fulvous hairstreak (*Electrostrymon angelia*)
Sky-blue groundstreak (*Kisutam syllis*)
Red-banded hairstreak (*Calycopis cecrops*)
Dusky-blue groundstreak (*Calycopis isobeon*)
Gray hairstreak (*Strymon melinus*)
Avalon scrub-hairstreak (*Strymon avalona*)
Red-crescent scrub-hairstreak (*Strymon rufofusca*)
White scrub-hairstreak (*Strymon albata*)
Lacey's scrub-hairstreak (*Strymon alea*)
Red-lined scrub-hairstreak (*Strymon bebrycia*)
Yojoa scrub-hairstreak (*Strymon yojoa*)
Tailless scrub-hairstreak (*Strymon cestri*)
Martial scrub-hairstreak (*Strymon martialis*)
Bartram's scrub-hairstreak (*Strymon acis*)
Lantana scrub-hairstreak (*Strymon bazochii*)
Mallow scrub-hairstreak (*Strymon istapa*)
Disguised scrub-hairstreak (*Strymon limenia*)
Bromeliad scrub-hairstreak (*Strymon serapio*)
Red-spotted hairstreak (*Tmolus echion*)
Leda ministreak (*Ministrymon leda*)
Clytie ministreak (*Ministrymon clytie*)
Gray ministreak (*Ministrymon azia*)
Pearly-gray hairstreak (*Strephonota tephraeus*)
White M hairstreak (*Parrhasius m-album*)
Sonoran hairstreak (*Hypostrymon critola*)
Early hairstreak (*Erora laeta*)
Arizona hairstreak (*Erora quaderna*)

Blues (Polyommatinae)
Pea blue (*Lampides boeticus*)
Cassius blue (*Leptotes cassius*)
Marine blue (*Leptotes marina*)
Western pygmy-blue (*Brephidium exilis*)
Eastern pygmy-blue (*Brephidium pseudofea*)
Lesser grass blue (*Zizina otis*)
Cyna blue (*Zizula cyna*)
Eastern tailed-blue (*Cupido comyntas*)
Western tailed-blue (*Cupido amyntula*)
Lucia azure (*Celastrina lucia*)
Pacific azure (*Celastrina echo*)
Spring azure (*Celastrina ladon*)
Holly azure (*Celastrina idella*)
Cherry gall azure (*Celastrina serotina*)
Summer azure (*Celastrina neglecta*)
Hops azure (*Celastrina humulus*)
Appalachian azure (*Celastrina neglectamajor*)
Dusky azure (*Celastrina nigra*)
Miami blue (*Cyclargus thomasi*)
Nickerbean blue (*Cyclargus ammon*)
Reakirt's blue (*Echinargus isola*)
Ceraunus blue (*Hemiargus ceraunus*)
Sonoran blue (*Philotes sonorensis*)
Small blue (*Philotiella speciosa*)
Leona's blue (*Philotiella leona*)
Square-spotted blue (*Euphilotes battoides*)
Glaucon blue (*Euphilotes glaucon*)
Central dotted-blue (*Euphilotes centralis*)
Bernardino blue (*Euphilotes bernardino*)

Ellis's blue (*Euphilotes ellisii*)
Bauer's blue (*Euphilotes baueri*)
Mojave dotted blue (*Euphilotes mojave*)
Stanford's blue (*Euphilotes stanfordorum*)
Dotted blue (*Euphilotes enoptes*)
Columbian blue (*Euphilotes columbiae*)
Ancilla blue (*Euphilotes ancilla*)
Rita's blue (*Euphilotes rita*)
Pallid blue (*Euphilotes pallescens*)
Spalding's blue (*Euphilotes spaldingi*)
Arrowhead blue (*Glaucopsyche piasus*)
Silvery blue (*Glaucopsyche lygdamus*)
Northern blue (*Plebejus idas*)
Anna's blue (*Plebejus anna*)
Karner blue (*Plebejus samuelis*)
Melissa blue (*Plebejus melissa*)
Friday's blue (*Plebejus fridayi*)
Greenish blue (*Plebejus saepiolus*)
San Emigdio blue (*Plebejus emigdionis*)
Boisduval's blue (*Plebejus icarioides*)
Shasta blue (*Plebejus shasta*)
Acmon blue (*Plebejus acmon*)
Lupine blue (*Plebejus lupini*)
Cotundra blue (*Plebejus cotundra*)
Veined blue (*Plebejus neurona*)
Cranberry blue (*Plebejus optilete*)
Arctic blue (*Plebejus glandon*)
Sierra blue (*Plebejus podarce*)
Common blue (*Polyommatus icarus*)

Metalmarks (Riodinidae)

True metalmarks (Riodinidae)
Northern metalmark (*Calephelis borealis*)
Swamp metalmark (*Calephelis muticum*)
Little metalmark (*Calephelis virginiensis*)
Fatal calephelis (*Calephelis nemesis*)
Rounded calephelis (*Calephelis perditalis*)
Wright's calephelis (*Calephelis wrighti*)
Rawson's calephelis (*Calephelis rawsoni*)
Freeman's calephelis (*Calephelis freemani*)
Arizona calephelis (*Calephelis arizonensis*)
Red-bordered metalmark (*Caria ino*)
Bumblebee metalmark (*Baeotis zonata*)
Blue lasaia (*Lasaia sula*)
Pixie (*Melanis pixe*)
Falcate emesis (*Emesis tenedia*)
Zela emesis (*Emesis zela*)
Ares emesis (*Emesis ares*)
Curve-winged emesis (*Emesis emesia*)
Mormon metalmark (*Apodemia mormo*)
Behr's metalmark (*Apodemia virgulti*)
Desert Mexican metalmark (*Apodemia mejicanus*)
Dury's metalmark (*Apodemia duryi*)
Palmer's metalmark (*Apodemia palmerii*)
Hepburn's metalmark (*Apodemia hepburni*)
Walker's metalmark (*Apodemia walkeri*)
Narrow-winged metalmark (*Apodemia multiplaga*)
Crescent metalmark (*Apodemia phyciodoides*)
Nais metalmark (*Apodemia nais*)
Chisos metalmark (*Apodemia chisosensis*)

Brushfoots (Nymphalidae)

Snouts (Libytheinae)
American snout (*Libytheana carinenta*)

Monarch and relatives (Danainae)
Monarch (*Danaus plexippus*)
Queen (*Danaus gilippus*)
Soldier (*Danaus eresimus*)
Tiger mimic-queen (*Lycorea halia*)

Actinotes, heliconians, and fritillaries (Heliconiinae)
Gulf fritillary (*Agraulis vanillae*)
Banded longwing (*Dryadula phaetusa*)
Julia (*Dryas iulia*)
Zebra longwing (*Heliconius charithonia*)
Crimson-patched longwing (*Heliconius erato*)
Variegated fritillary (*Euptoieta claudia*)
Mexican fritillary (*Euptoieta hegesia*)
Mountain fritillary (*Boloria alaskensis*)
Bog fritillary (*Boloria eunomia*)
Silver-bordered fritillary (*Boloria selene*)
Meadow fritillary (*Boloria bellona*)
Frigga fritillary (*Boloria frigga*)
Dingy fritillary (*Boloria improba*)
Relict fritillary (*Boloria kriemhild*)
Pacific fritillary (*Boloria epithore*)
Polaris fritillary (*Boloria polaris*)
Alberta fritillary (*Boloria alberta*)
Astarte fritillary (*Boloria astarte*)
Freija fritillary (*Boloria freija*)
Cryptic fritillary (*Boloria natazhati*)
Purplish fritillary (*Boloria chariclea*)
Diana fritillary (*Speyeria diana*)
Great spangled fritillary (*Speyeria cybele*)
Aphrodite fritillary (*Speyeria aphrodite*)
Regal fritillary (*Speyeria idalia*)
Nokomis fritillary (*Speyeria nokomis*)
Edwards's fritillary (*Speyeria edwardsii*)
Coronis fritillary (*Speyeria coronis*)
Carol's fritillary (*Speyeria carolae*)
Zerene fritillary (*Speyeria zerene*)
Callippe fritillary (*Speyeria callippe*)
Great Basin fritillary (*Speyeria egleis*)
Unsilvered fritillary (*Speyeria adiaste*)
Atlantis fritillary (*Speyeria atlantis*)
Northwestern fritillary (*Speyeria hesperis*)
Hydaspe fritillary (*Speyeria hydaspe*)
Mormon fritillary (*Speyeria mormonia*)

Sisters and admirals (Limenitidinae)
White admiral (*Limenitis arthemis*)
Red-spotted purple (*Limenitis arthemis*)
Weidemeyer's admiral (*Limenitis weidemeyerii*)
Lorquin's admiral (*Limenitis lorquini*)
Viceroy (*Limenitis archippus*)
Arizona sister (*Adelpha eulalia*)
California sister (*Adelpha californica*)
Band-celled sister (*Adelpha fessonia*)
Spot-celled sister (*Adelpha basiloides*)

Emperors (Apaturinae)
Hackberry emperor (*Asterocampa celtis*)
Empress Leilia (*Asterocampa leilia*)
Tawny emperor (*Asterocampa clyton*)
Dusky emperor (*Asterocampa idyja*)
Pavon emperor (*Doxocopa pavon*)
Silver emperor (*Doxocopa laure*)

Exotic brushfoots (Biblidinae)
Red rim (*Biblis hyperia*)
Northern mestra (*Mestra amymone*)
Florida purplewing (*Eunica tatila*)
Dingy purplewing (*Eunica monima*)
Blackened bluewing (*Myscelia cyananthe*)
Mexican bluewing (*Myscelia ethusa*)
Gray cracker (*Hamadryas februa*)
Caribbean cracker (*Hamadryas amphichloe*)
Glaucous cracker (*Hamadryas glauconome*)
Variable cracker (*Hamadryas feronia*)
Guatamalan cracker (*Hamadryas guatemalena*)
Brownish cracker (*Hamadryas iphthime*)
Common banner (*Epiphile adrasta*)
Orange banner (*Temenis laothoe*)
Mexican sailor (*Dynamine postverta*)
Blue-eyed sailor (*Dynamine dyonis*)

185

Complete List of North American Butterflies

Daggerwings (Cyrestinae)
Many-banded daggerwing (*Marpesia chiron*)
Ruddy daggerwing (*Marpesia petreus*)
Caribbean daggerwing (*Marpesia eleuchea*)
Waiter daggerwing (*Marpesia zerynthia*)

True brushfoots (Nymphalinae)
Orion cecropian (*Historis odius*)
Blomfild's beauty (*Smyrna blomfildia*)
Orange mapwing (*Hypanartia lethe*)
West Coast lady (*Vanessa annabella*)
Red admiral (*Vanessa atalanta*)
Kameamea (*Vanessa tameamea*)
Milbert's tortoiseshell (*Aglais milberti*)
Compton tortoiseshell (*Nymphalis l-album*)
California tortoiseshell (*Nymphalis californica*)
Mourning cloak (*Nymphalis antiopa*)
Question mark (*Polygonia interrogationis*)
Comma anglewing (*Polygonia comma*)
Satyr anglewing (*Polygonia satyrus*)
Gray anglewing (*Polygonia progne*)
Oreas anglewing (*Polygonia oreas*)
Hoary anglewing (*Polygonia gracilis*)
Green anglewing (*Polygonia faunus*)
White peacock (*Anartia jatrophae*)
Banded peacock (*Anartia fatima*)
Cuban peacock (*Anartia chrysopelea*)
Malachite (*Siproeta stelenes*)
Rusty-tipped page (*Siproeta epaphus*)
Northern buckeye (*Junonia coenia*)
Dark buckeye (*Junonia evarete*)
Mangrove buckeye (*Junonia genoveva*)
Mimic (*Hypolimnas misippus*)
Gillette's checkerspot (*Euphydryas gillettii*)
Edith's checkerspot (*Euphydryas editha*)
Chalcedon checkerspot (*Euphydryas chalcedona*)
Snowberry checkerspot (*Euphydryas colon*)
Anicia checkerspot (*Euphydryas anicia*)
Baltimore checkerspot (*Euphydryas phaeton*)
Dotted checkerspot (*Poladryas minuta*)
Arachne checkerspot (*Poladryas arachne*)
Crimson-patch checkerspot (*Chlosyne janais*)
Definite checkerspot (*Chlosyne definita*)
Melitaeoides checkerspot (*Chlosyne melitaeoides*)
Banded checkerspot (*Chlosyne endeis*)
Rosita checkerspot (*Chlosyne rosita*)
Theona checkerspot (*Chlosyne theona*)
Cyneas checkerspot (*Chlosyne cyneas*)
Fulvia checkerspot (*Chlosyne fulvia*)
Leanira checkerspot (*Chlosyne leanira*)
Silvery checkerspot (*Chlosyne nycteis*)
Gorgone checkerspot (*Chlosyne gorgone*)
California patch (*Chlosyne californica*)
Bordered patch (*Chlosyne lacinia*)
Harris's checkerspot (*Chlosyne harrisii*)
Hoffmann's checkerspot (*Chlosyne hoffmanni*)
Sierra Nevada checkerspot (*Chlosyne whitneyi*)
Sagebrush checkerspot (*Chlosyne acastus*)
Gabb's checkerspot (*Chlosyne gabbii*)
Northern checkerspot (*Chlosyne palla*)
Rockslide checkerspot (*Chlosyne damoetas*)
Elf (*Microtia elva*)
Tiny checkerspot (*Dymasia dymas*)
Arizona checkerspot (*Texola elada*)
Elada checkerspot (*Texola elada*)
Black-bordered crescent (*Tegosa luka*)
Texan crescent (*Anthanassa texana*)
Chestnut crescent (*Anthanassa argentea*)
Cuban crescent (*Anthanassa frisia*)
Pale-banded crescent (*Anthanassa tulcis*)
Vesta crescent (*Phyciodes graphica*)
Painted crescent (*Phyciodes picta*)
California crescent (*Phyciodes orseis*)
Pale crescent (*Phyciodes pallida*)
Mylitta crescent (*Phyciodes mylitta*)

Phaon crescent (*Phyciodes phaon*)
Pearl crescent (*Phyciodes tharos*)
Northern crescent (*Phyciodes cocyta*)
Tawny crescent (*Phyciodes batesii*)
Field crescent (*Phyciodes pulchella*)

Leafwings and relatives (Charaxinae)
Florida leafwing (*Anaea troglodyta*)
Tropical leafwing (*Anaea aidea*)
Goatweed leafwing (*Anaea andria*)
Cuban leafwing (*Memphis echemus*)
Pale-spotted leafwing (*Memphis pithyusa*)
Forrer's leafwing (*Memphis forreri*)
One-spotted prepona (*Archeoprepona demophon*)

Satyrs (Satyrinae)
Southern pearly-eye (*Lethe portlandia*)
Northern pearly-eye (*Lethe anthedon*)
Creole pearly-eye (*Lethe creola*)
Eyed brown (*Lethe eurydice*)
Appalachian brown (*Lethe appalachia*)
Hayden's ringlet (*Coenonympha haydenii*)
Common ringlet (*Coenonympha tullia*)
Nabokov's satyr (*Cyllopsis pyracmon*)
Canyonland gemmed-satyr (*Cyllopsis pertepida*)
Eastern gemmed-satyr (*Cyllopsis gemma*)
Arizona pine-satyr (*Paramacera xicaque*)
Mexican pine-satyr (*Paramacera xicaque*)
Georgia satyr (*Neonympha areolatus*)
Helicta satyr (*Neonympha helicta*)
Mitchell's satyr (*Neonympha mitchellii*)
Little wood-satyr (*Megisto cymela*)
Red satyr (*Megisto rubricata*)
Hermes satyr (*Hermeuptychia hermes*)
Carolina satyr (*Hermeuptychia sosybius*)
Vidler's alpine (*Erebia vidleri*)
Ross's alpine (*Erebia rossii*)
Disa alpine (*Erebia disa*)
Taiga alpine (*Erebia mancinus*)
Magdalena alpine (*Erebia magdalena*)
Mt. McKinley alpine (*Erebia mackinleyensis*)
Banded alpine (*Erebia fasciata*)
Common alpine (*Erebia epipsodea*)
Red-disked alpine (*Erebia discoidalis*)
Theano alpine (*Erebia pawloskii*)
Young's alpine (*Erebia youngi*)
Lafontaine's alpine (*Erebia lafontainei*)
Eskimo alpine (*Erebia occulta*)
Colorado alpine (*Erebia callias*)
Ridings' satyr (*Neominois ridingsii*)
Philip's arctic (*Oeneis philipi*)
Polixenes arctic (*Oeneis polixenes*)
Jutta arctic (*Oeneis jutta*)
Melissa arctic (*Oeneis melissa*)
Sentinel arctic (*Oeneis alpina*)
White-veined arctic (*Oeneis bore*)
Chryxus arctic (*Oeneis chryxus*)
Alberta arctic (*Oeneis alberta*)
Great arctic (*Oeneis nevadensis*)
Macoun's arctic (*Oeneis macounii*)
Uhler's arctic (*Oeneis uhleri*)
Common wood-nymph (*Cercyonis pegala*)
Mead's wood-nymph (*Cercyonis meadii*)
Great Basin wood-nymph (*Cercyonis sthenele*)
Small wood-nymph (*Cercyonis oetus*)
Red-bordered satyr (*Gyrocheilus patrobas*)

Skippers (Hesperiidae)

Spreadwing skippers (Eudaminae)
Guava skipper (*Phocides polybius*)
Belus skipper (*Phocides belus*)
Mangrove skipper (*Phocides pigmalion*)
Mercurial skipper (*Proteides mercurius*)

Zestos skipper (*Epargyreus zestos*)
"California" silver-spotted skipper (*Epargyreus clarus*)
Broken silverdrop (*Epargyreus exadeus*)
Hammock skipper (*Polygonus leo*)
Manuel's skipper (*Polygonus savigny*)
White-striped longtail (*Chioides albofasciatus*)
Zilpa longtail (*Chioides zilpa*)
Gold-spotted aguna (*Aguna asander*)
Emerald aguna (*Aguna claxon*)
Long-tailed aguna (*Aguna metophis*)
Mottled longtail (*Typhedanus undulatus*)
Eight-spotted longtail (*Polythrix octomaculata*)
Mexican longtail (*Polythrix mexicanus*)
Short-tailed skipper (*Zestusa dorus*)
White-crescent mottled-skipper (*Codatractus alcaeus*)
Arizona mottled-skipper (*Codatractus arizonensis*)
Valeriana skipper (*Codatractus valeriana*)
Long-tailed skipper (*Urbanus proteus*)
Bell's longtail (*Urbanus belli*)
Pronus longtail (*Urbanus pronus*)
Esmeralda longtail (*Urbanus esmeraldus*)
Dorantes longtail (*Urbanus dorantes*)
Brown longtail (*Urbanus procne*)
Plain longtail (*Urbanus simplicius*)
Teleus longtail (*Urbanus teleus*)
Tanna longtail (*Urbanus tanna*)
White-tailed longtail (*Urbanus doryssus*)
Small-spotted flasher (*Astraptes egregius*)
Frosted flasher (*Astraptes alardus*)
Gilbert's flasher (*Astraptes alector*)
Yellow-tipped flasher (*Astraptes anaphus*)
Golden banded-skipper (*Autochton cellus*)
Sonoran banded-skipper (*Autochton pseudocellus*)
Chisos banded-skipper (*Autochton cincta*)
Hoary edge (*Achalarus lyciades*)
Desert cloudywing (*Achalarus casica*)
White-edged cloudywing (*Achalarus albociliatus*)
Coyote cloudywing (*Achalarus toxeus*)
Jalapus cloudywing (*Thessia jalapus*)
Drusius cloudywing (*Thorybes drusius*)
Southern cloudywing (*Thorybes bathyllus*)
Northern cloudywing (*Thorybes pylades*)
Confused cloudywing (*Thorybes confusis*)
Western cloudywing (*Thorybes diversus*)
Mexican cloudywing (*Thorybes mexicana*)
Potrillo skipper (*Cabares potrillo*)
Falcate skipper (*Spathilepia clonius*)
Mimosa skipper (*Cogia calchas*)
Acacia skipper (*Cogia hippalus*)
Outis skipper (*Cogia outis*)
Gold-costa skipper (*Cogia caicus*)

Spreadwing skippers (Pyrginae)
"Arizona" araxes skipper (*Apyrrothrix araxes*)
Fritzgaertner's flat (*Celaenorrhinus fritzgaertneri*)
Stallings' flat (*Celaenorrhinus stallingsi*)
Starred skipper (*Arteurotia tractipennis*)
Purplish tufted-skipper (*Nisoniades rubescens*)
Glazed tufted-skipper (*Pellicia arina*)
Morning glory tufted-skipper (*Pellicia dimidiata*)
Wind's skipper (*Windia windi*)
Red-studded skipper (*Noctuana stator*)
Obscure sootywing (*Bolla brennus*)
Mottled sootywing (*Bolla clytius*)
Golden-headed sootywing (*Staphylus ceos*)
Hayhurst's scallopwing (*Staphylus hayhurstii*)
Mazans sootywing (*Staphylus mazans*)
Common sootywing (*Pholisora catullus*)
Mexican sootywing (*Pholisora mejicanus*)
Saltbush sootywing (*Hesperopsis alpheus*)
MacNeill's sootywing (*Hesperopsis gracielae*)
Mojave sootywing (*Hesperopsis libya*)
Variegated skipper (*Gorgythion begga*)
Pale mylon (*Mylon pelopidas*)
Hermit skipper (*Grais stigmaticus*)

Brown-banded skipper (*Timochares ruptifasciata*)
Common anastrus (*Anastrus sempiternus*)
White-patched skipper (*Chiomara georgina*)
Mithrax duskywing (*Chiomara mithrax*)
False duskywing (*Gesta invisus*)
Florida duskywing (*Ephyriades brunnea*)
Dreamy duskywing (*Erynnis icelus*)
Sleepy duskywing (*Erynnis brizo*)
Juvenal's duskywing (*Erynnis juvenalis*)
Rocky Mountain duskywing (*Erynnis telemachus*)
Meridian duskywing (*Erynnis meridianus*)
Scudder's duskywing (*Erynnis scudderi*)
Horace's duskywing (*Erynnis horatius*)
Mournful duskywing (*Erynnis tristis*)
Mexican mournful duskywing (*Erynnis tristis*)
Mottled duskywing (*Erynnis martialis*)
Pacuvius duskywing (*Erynnis pacuvius*)
Zarucco duskywing (*Erynnis zarucco*)
Funereal duskywing (*Erynnis funeralis*)
Wild indigo duskywing (*Erynnis baptisiae*)
Columbine duskywing (*Erynnis lucilius*)
Afranius duskywing (*Erynnis afranius*)
Persius duskywing (*Erynnis persius*)
Pale sicklewing (*Achlyodes pallida*)
Northern sicklewing (sickle-winged skipper)
    (*Eantis tamenund*)
Common spurwing (*Antigonus erosus*)
White spurwing (*Antigonus emorsa*)
Texas powdered-skipper (*Systasea pulverulenta*)
Arizona powdered-skipper (*Systasea zampa*)
Common streaky-skipper (*Celotes nessus*)
West Texas streaky-skipper (*Celotes limpia*)
Grizzled skipper (*Pyrgus centaureae*)
Two-banded checkered-skipper (*Pyrgus ruralis*)
Mountain checkered-skipper (*Pyrgus xanthus*)
Small checkered-skipper (*Pyrgus scriptura*)
Common checkered-skipper (*Pyrgus communis*)
White checkered-skipper (*Pyrgus albescens*)
Tropical checkered-skipper (*Pyrgus oileus*)
Desert checkered-skipper (*Pyrgus philetas*)
Erichson's white-skipper (*Heliopyrgus domicella*)
East Mexican white-skipper (*Heliopyrgus sublinea*)
Northern white-skipper (*Heliopetes ericetorum*)
Laviana white-skipper (*Heliopetes laviana*)
Turk's-cap white-skipper (*Heliopetes macaira*)
Veined white-skipper (*Heliopetes arsalte*)

Skipperlings (Heteropterinae)
Arctic skipperling (*Carterocephalus palaemon*)
Russet skipperling (*Piruna pirus*)
Chisos skipperling (*Piruna haferniki*)
Hour-glass skipperling (*Piruna penaea*)
Four-spotted skipperling (*Piruna polingii*)

Grass-skippers (Hesperiinae)
Banana skipper (*Erionota thrax*)
Green-backed ruby-eye (*Perichares adela*)
Yucca giant-skipper (*Megathymus yuccae*)
Ursine giant-skipper (*Megathymus ursus*)
Cofaqui giant-skipper (*Megathymus cofaqui*)
Strecker's giant-skipper (*Megathymus streckeri*)
Manfreda giant-skipper (*Stallingsia maculosus*)
Neumoegen's giant-skipper (*Agathymus neumoegeni*)
Poling's giant-skipper (*Agathymus polingi*)
Huachuca giant-skipper (*Agathymus evansi*)
Arizona giant-skipper (*Agathymus aryxna*)
Bauer's giant-skipper (*Agathymus baueri*)
Gentry's giant-skipper (*Agathymus gentryi*)
Mary's giant-skipper (*Agathymus mariae*)
Gilbert's giant-skipper (*Agathymus gilberti*)
Estelle's giant-skipper (*Agathymus estelleae*)
California giant-skipper (*Agathymus stephensi*)
Mojave giant-skipper (*Agathymus alliae*)
Least skipper (*Ancyloxypha numitor*)
Tropical least skipper (*Ancyloxypha arene*)

Poweshiek skipperling (*Oarisma poweshiek*)
Garita skipperling (*Oarisma garita*)
Edwards' skipperling (*Oarisma edwardsii*)
Orange skipperling (*Copaeodes aurantiaca*)
Southern skipperling (*Copaeodes minima*)
Sunrise skipper (*Adopaeoides prittwitzi*)
European skipper (*Thymelicus lineola*)
Brazilian skipper (*Calpodes ethlius*)
Salt marsh skipper (*Panoquina panoquin*)
Obscure skipper (*Panoquina panoquinoides*)
Wandering skipper (*Panoquina errans*)
Hecebolus skipper (*Panoquina hecebolus*)
Purple-washed skipper (*Panoquina lucas*)
Evans' skipper (*Panoquina evansi*)
Northern faceted-skipper (*Synapte pecta*)
Salenus faceted-skipper (*Synapte salenus*)
Redundant skipper (*Corticea corticea*)
Large roadside-skipper (*Amblyscirtes exoteria*)
Cassus roadside-skipper (*Amblyscirtes cassus*)
Texas roadside-skipper (*Amblyscirtes texanae*)
Bronze roadside-skipper (*Amblyscirtes aenus*)
Linda's roadside-skipper (*Amblyscirtes linda*)
Oslar's roadside-skipper (*Amblyscirtes oslari*)
Elissa roadside-skipper (*Amblyscirtes elissa*)
Pepper and salt skipper (*Amblyscirtes hegon*)
Carolina roadside-skipper (*Amblyscirtes carolina*)
Reversed roadside-skipper (*Amblyscirtes reversa*)
Lace-winged roadside-skipper (*Amblyscirtes aesculapius*)
Slaty roadside-skipper (*Amblyscirtes nereus*)
Nysa roadside-skipper (*Amblyscirtes nysa*)
Dotted roadside-skipper (*Amblyscirtes eos*)
Common roadside-skipper (*Amblyscirtes vialis*)
Dusky roadside-skipper (*Amblyscirtes alternata*)
Celia's roadside-skipper (*Amblyscirtes celia*)
Bell's roadside-skipper (*Amblyscirtes belli*)
Toltec roadside-skipper (*Amblyscirtes tolteca*)
Orange-headed roadside-skipper (*Amblyscirtes phylace*)
Pale-rayed skipper (*Vidius perigenes*)
Swarthy skipper (*Nastra lherminier*)
Neamathla skipper (*Nastra neamathla*)
Julia's skipper (*Nastra julia*)
Three-spotted skipper (*Cymaenes tripunctus*)
Fawn-spotted skipper (*Cymaenes trebius*)
Eufala skipper (*Lerodea eufala*)
Violet-clouded skipper (*Lerodea arabus*)
Clouded skipper (*Lerema accius*)
Fantastic skipper (*Vettius fantasos*)
Osca skipper (*Rhinthon osca*)
Fiery skipper (*Hylephila phyleus*)
Alkali skipper (*Pseudocopaeodes eunus*)
Uncas skipper (*Hesperia uncas*)
Juba skipper (*Hesperia juba*)
Common branded skipper (*Hesperia comma*)
Plains branded skipper (*Hesperia assiniboia*)
Western branded skipper (*Hesperia colorado*)
Apache skipper (*Hesperia woodgatei*)
Ottoe skipper (*Hesperia ottoe*)
Leonard's skipper (*Hesperia leonardus*)
Pahaska skipper (*Hesperia pahaska*)
Columbian skipper (*Hesperia columbia*)
Cobweb skipper (*Hesperia metea*)
Green skipper (*Hesperia viridis*)
Dotted skipper (*Hesperia attalus*)
Meske's skipper (*Hesperia meskei*)
Dakota skipper (*Hesperia dacotae*)
Lindsey's skipper (*Hesperia lindseyi*)
Indian skipper (*Hesperia sassacus*)
Sierra skipper (*Hesperia miriamae*)
Nevada skipper (*Hesperia nevada*)
Rhesus skipper (*Polites rhesus*)
Carus skipper (*Polites carus*)
Peck's skipper (*Polites peckius*)
Sandhill skipper (*Polites sabuleti*)
Draco skipper (*Polites draco*)
Mardon skipper (*Polites mardon*)

Tawny-edged skipper (*Polites themistocles*)
Baracoa skipper (*Polites baracoa*)
Crossline skipper (*Polites origenes*)
Long dash (*Polites mystic*)
Sonoran skipper (*Polites sonora*)
Whirlabout (*Polites vibex*)
Northern broken-dash (*Wallengrenia egeremet*)
Southern broken-dash (*Wallengrenia otho*)
Little glassywing (*Pompeius verna*)
Sachem (*Atalopedes campestris*)
Arogos skipper (*Atrytone arogos*)
Byssus skipper (*Problema byssus*)
Rare skipper (*Problema bulenta*)
Hobomok skipper (*Poanes hobomok*)
Zabulon skipper (*Poanes zabulon*)
Taxiles skipper (*Poanes taxiles*)
Mulberry wing (*Poanes massasoit*)
Broad-winged skipper (*Poanes viator*)
Aaron's skipper (*Poanes aaroni*)
Yehl skipper (*Poanes yehl*)
Umber skipper (*Poanes melane*)
Morrison's skipper (*Stinga morrisoni*)
Woodland skipper (*Ochlodes sylvanoides*)
Rural skipper (*Ochlodes agricola*)
Yuma skipper (*Ochlodes yuma*)
Snow's skipper (*Paratrytone snowi*)
Delaware skipper (*Anatrytone logan*)
De la Maza's skipper (*Anatrytone mazai*)
Common mellana (*Quasimellana eulogius*)
Simius skipper (*Notamblyscirtes simius*)
Palatka skipper (*Euphyes pilatka*)
Black dash (*Euphyes conspicua*)
Berry's skipper (*Euphyes berryi*)
Bay skipper (*Euphyes bayensis*)
Dion skipper (*Euphyes dion*)
Dukes' skipper (*Euphyes dukesi*)
Two-spotted skipper (*Euphyes bimacula*)
Palmetto skipper (*Euphyes arpa*)
Dun skipper (*Euphyes vestris*)
Double-dotted skipper (*Decinea percosius*)
Twin-spot skipper (*Oligoria maculata*)
Dusted skipper (*Atrytonopsis hianna*)
Loamm's skipper (*Atrytonopsis loammi*)
Deva skipper (*Atrytonopsis deva*)
Moon-marked skipper (*Atrytonopsis lunus*)
Viereck's skipper (*Atrytonopsis vierecki*)
White-barred skipper (*Atrytonopsis pittacus*)
Python skipper (*Atrytonopsis python*)
Cestus skipper (*Atrytonopsis cestus*)
Sheep skipper (*Atrytonopsis edwardsi*)
Chestnut-marked skipper (*Thespieus macareus*)

Further Reading

Books

Allen, Thomas J., Jim P. Brock, and J. Glassberg. *Caterpillars in the Field and Garden.* Oxford University Press, 2005.

Bailowitz, Richard A., and J. P. Brock. *Butterflies of Southeastern Arizona.* Sonoran Arthropod Studies Inc., 1990.

Bird, C. D., G. J. Hilchie, N. G. Kondla, E. M. Pike, and F. A. H. Sperling. *Butterflies of Alberta.* Provincial Museum of Alberta, 1995.

Brock, Jim P., and Kenn Kaufman. *Kaufman Field Guide to Butterflies of North America.* Houghton Mifflin Company, 2003.

Ferris, C. D., and F. M. Brown. *Butterflies of the Rocky Mountain States.* University of Oklahoma Press, 1981.

Glassberg, Jeffrey. *Butterflies through Binoculars: The East.* Oxford University Press, 1999.

ibid., Butterflies through Binoculars: The West. Oxford University Press, 2001.

Guppy, Crispin S., and Jon H. Shepard. *Butterflies of British Columbia.* University of British Columbia Press, 2001.

Heath, Fred. *Introduction to Southern California Butterflies.* Mountain Press Publishing Company, 2004.

Layberry, Ross A., Peter W. Hall, and J. Donald Lafontaine. *The Butterflies of Canada.* University of Toronto Press, 1998.

Minno, Marc C., Jerry F. Butler, and Donald W. Hall. *Florida Butterfly Caterpillars and Their Host Plants.* University Press of Florida, 2005.

Monroe, Lynn, and Gene Monroe. *Butterflies and Their Favorite Flowering Plants of Anza-Borrego Desert State Park and Environs.* Merryleaf Press, 2004.

Opler, Paul A. *A Field Guide to Eastern Butterflies.* Houghton Mifflin Company, 1998.

ibid., A Field Guide to Western Butterflies. Houghton Mifflin Company, 1999.

Pyle, Robert. *Mariposa Road: the Firsts Butterfly Big Year.* Houghton Mifflin Harcourt, 2010.

ibid., The Butterflies of Cascadia. Seattle Audubon Society, 2002.

Scott, James. *The Butterflies of North America: A Natural History and Field Guide.* Stanford University Press, 1992.

Shapiro, A. M., and T. D. Manolis. *Field Guide to Butterflies of the San Francisco Bay and Sacramento Valley Regions.* University of California Press, 2007.

Stewart, Bob, Priscilla Brodkin, and Hank Brodkin. *Butterflies of Arizona: A Photographic Guide.* West Coast Lady Press, 2001.

Wauer, Roland H. *Finding Butterflies in Texas.* Spring Creek Press, 2006.

Weber, Larry. *Butterflies of New England.* Kollath-Stensaas Publishing, 2002.

DVDs

Ebner, J.A., and P.A. Opler. *Audubon Videoguide to Butterflies: Essentials for Beginners and Gardeners*. Mastervision, 2008.

Ebner, J.A., and P.A. Opler. *Audubon Videoguide to Butterflies: Common & Endangered*. Mastervision, 2009.

Web sites

Butterflies and Moths of North America
http://butterfliesandmoths.org/

Butterflies of America
http://butterfliesofamerica.com/

Butterflies of Canada
http://www.cbif.gc.ca/spp_pages/butterflies/index_e.php

Butterflies of Southeastern Arizona
http://nitro.biosci.arizona.edu/zEEB/butterflies/seazlist.html

Butterflies of the Northern Colorado Front Range
http://www.coloradofrontrangebutterflies.com/

The Children's Butterfly Site
http://www.kidsbutterfly.org/

Monarch Watch, University of Kansas Society
http://www.monarchwatch.org/

North American Butterfly Association
http://www.naba.org/

Art Shapiro's Butterfly Site
http://butterfly.ucdavis.edu/

Wisconsin Butterflies
http://wisconsinbutterflies.org/

Index

Page numbers in *italics* refer to images.

190

191

Picture Credits

2: Richard Skoonberg. 6: Roger Manrique Molina. 7: Sebastien Rigault (www.flickr.com/photos/sebjen). 8: Betty Ramsey. 9: Liliana Ramírez-Freire. 10: John Villella. Page 11: Bill Bouton. Page 12: Guadalupe Fernandez. 13: Susan Ford Collins. 16: Tony Adcock. 17: Mary Funderburk. 18: David Trently. 20: Caleb Sconosciuto. 21: Jim Gagnon (MNIrisguy). 22: Alberto. 23: Anne Toal. 24 (top): David Raby. 24 (bottom): Tanya Puntti. 25: Jim Gilbert. 26: Eddie Nurcombe. 28: João P. Burini. 29 (top): Sharon Mollerus. 29 (bottom): Ken Pomerance (Mr. Clean Photography). 30: Antony Scott. 31: Bill Bouton. 32: dasaan_uk. 33: Douglass Moody. 34–35: Diane P. Brooks. 36: David R. Guzman. 37 (top): Tim Lindenbaum. 37 (bottom): Adrian Jones. 38: James W. Petranka. 39: Dean Morley. 40: Tyler Bryce Fox. 41: Matt Steinhausen. 42: Eric Heupel. 43: Dean Morley. 45: Harry P. Hunt. 46: Curt Hart. 47: Tim Hoeflich. 48: Brad Smith. 49: Inge Helene Nørgaard. 50: Dean Morley. 51 (top): Julie A. Craves. 51 (bottom): Dean Morley. 52: Kevin Schafer/Corbis. 53: Brad Smith. 54: Michael Jefferies. 55: Margrit Struck. 56: Anne Toal. 57: Annie Griffiths/Corbis. 58–59: Keith Dannemiller/Corbis. 60: Dwight Sipler (www.flickr.com/photos/photofarmer/). 61: Jean Sinclair/Getty. 62: Eugene Zelenko, CC-BY-SA. 63: N. Vivienne Shen Photography/Getty. 64: Kevin Arvin. 65: Dean Morley. 66: Jim McCulloch. 67: Carmen Phillips. 68: Roy Brown Photography. 69: Bill Swindaman. 70: James C. Winner. 71: David Trently. 72: Curt Hart. 73: Daniel P. McKiernan. 74: Kevin Wan. 75: Ray Bruun. 76: Patrick Coin. 77: Patricia Garner. 78: Lauren Sobkoviak. 79: Ron Wolf. 80: Kayoko Y. Teele. 81: Ignazio Corda. 82: Jim McCulloch. 83: Ray Bruun. 84–85: Rob Santry. 86–87: Christian Nunes. 88: Alan Schmierer. 89: Tripp Davenport. 90: Clifford G. Powell. 91: Mark Rainey. 92: Jim McCulloch. 93–94: Curt Hart. 95: Frank Model (fsmodel@aol.com). 96: Anthony Gould. 97: Rob Santry. 98–99: Patrick Coin. 100: Jerry E. Shelton. 101: Rob Santry. 102: Ryan Rasmussen. 103: Mark Rainey. 104: David Beaudette. 105: Mark Rainey. 106: Ryan Shaw. 107: Fred M. Kahan. 108: Mark Rainey. 109: Timothy J. Fenske. 110: Alain Maire. 111–113: Rob Santry. 114: Bill Bouton. 115: Ryan Rasmussen. 116: Carolien Nieuwenhof Jacobs. 117: Bill Bouton. 118: Paul A. Opler. 119: Bill Bouton. 120: Ray Bruun. 121: Bill Bouton. 122: Anne Toal. 123: Anne Elliott. 124–125: Roy Brown Photography. 126: Curt Hart. 127: Jim McCulloch. 128: Anne Elliott. 129: Frank Model (fsmodel@aol.com). 130–131: Jim McCulloch. 132: Patrick Coin. 133: Jim McCulloch. 134: Patrick Coin. 135: Curt Hart. 136: Frank Model (fsmodel@aol.com). 137: Ray Bruun. 138: Bill Bouton. 139: James Lofton. 140: Mark Rainey. 141: Ron Wolf. 142: Mirella Zeeders. 143: Dean Morley. 144: Bron Praslicka. 145: Danny de Veen (dnnya17). 146–147: Aleta A. Rodriguez. 148: Steven R. House. 149: Li Wing. 150–151: Bill Bouton. 152: Peter Woods, courtesy of the Western Pennsylvania Conservancy. 153: Curt Hart. 154: Timothy J. Fenske. 155: Bill Bouton. 156–157: Curt Hart. 158: Jim McCulloch. 159: Patricia Garner. 160: Dave Rogers. 161: Curt Hart. 162: Jeff Trei. 163: Graham Toal. 164: Elizabeth A. Sellers. 165–166: Bill Bouton. 167: Tom Smith. 168: Bill Bouton. 169: Doug Waylett. 170: Bill Bouton. 171: Paul A. Opler. 172: Bill Bumgarner. 173: Eric R. Eaton. 174: John Varoumas. 175: Alain Maire. 176: Bill Bouton. 177: Alan Schmierer. 178: David Edwards (www.flickr.com/photos/dhedwards/). 179: Richard Skoonberg. 180: Bruce Campbell Bolin. 181: David Trently. 182: Mark Rainey. 183: Richard Stickney.